FLORIDA'S HISTORIC RESTAURANTS

and their recipes

FLORIDA'S HISTORIC RESTAURANTS

and their recipes

by DAWN O'BRIEN
AND BECKY ROPER MATKOV

Drawings by Debra Long Hampton

Revised Edition, 1994

Library of Congress Cataloging-in-Publication Data

O'Brien, Dawn.
Florida's historic restaurants and their recipes / by Dawn O'Brien
and Becky Matkov; drawings by Debra L. Hampton.
p.   cm.
Includes index.
ISBN 0-89587-120-3
1. Cookery, American—Southern style.   2. Cookery—Florida.
3. Restaurants, lunch rooms, etc.—Florida—Guide-books.
4. Historic buildings—Florida.   I. Matkov, Becky.   II. Title.
TX715.02827   1987   87–26540
641.509759—dc19

DEDICATION

My part of this book is dedicated to Joseph Collins, who believes that young women deserve an education, too.

Dawn O'Brien

To my friends across the state of Florida who have shared their personal recommendations and dining experiences with me; to my husband, Tom, for his support all these years; to my son, Tom, and my daughter, Grimsley, for surviving yet another of their mother's whirlwind projects.

Becky Roper Matkov

ACKNOWLEDGMENTS

Florida offers a whole spectrum of historic restaurants. The state that people think of as "variety vacationland" has not taken a vacation from preserving its past. There were many devoted native and adopted Floridians who uncovered paths for us during the researching, writing, and rewriting of the original and revised editions of this book. To those people, we owe a special debt of thanks. A big thank you to the following:

To: Katherine Keith, public-relations representative in Tourism and Public Relations for the Florida Department of Commerce.

To: The Florida county tourism development councils, chambers of commerce, and promotion agencies, and especially to Joanna Krumsieg at The Zimmerman Agency, F. Diane Pickett, president of The Turn Around Society in DeFuniak Springs, and Susie Nunnelley of Destin.

To: The Florida Trust for Historic Preservation, especially Mary Barrow, Jean Bunch, Bud Frazier, Sallye Jude, Tavia McCuean, and the late Ralph Renick.

To: The Florida Historic Preservation Advisory Council, especially former members Katharine Dickenson, Joan Jennewein, Roy Hunt, Marcia Lindstrom, and Don Slesnick.

To: Tampa Preservation, Inc., especially Frances Kruse and Harriet Plyler.

To: Dade Heritage Trust staff and board members, past and present.

To: The Historic Preservation Committee of the Junior League of Miami, Inc., especially Liz Bishop and Anna Ehlert.

To: Leslie Rivera of the Vizcayan Foundation.

To: Bill Branan, former executive director of Florida Defenders of the Environment.

To: George Sandora of the Gallery at Cedar Key.

To: Bob Jensen of the Elizabeth Ordway Dunn Foundation.

To: Blair Reeves, professor emeritus of the University of Florida School of Architecture.

To: Herb Hiller, author of the *Guide to the Small and Historic Lodgings of Florida*.

To: Arlene Commings of the Florida Main Street Program in Sebring.

To: Cookie O'Brien of the St. Augustine Historic Preservation Board.

To: Sherry Davich of Orlando Landmarks Defense, Inc.

To: Leadership Florida Network members Rick Edmonds, Allison DeFoor, Geoffrey Simon, and Ron Saunders.

To: Gloria Anderson, former editor of *Miami Today* newspaper.

To: The restaurateurs who shared their restaurants' heritage and the chefs who shared their time and talents.

To: The artist Debra Hampton, for such beautiful renderings.

To: The many guinea pigs who continue to taste and appreciate each state's culinary benefits.

FOREWORD

"Let them eat pizza!" was my collaborator Becky Roper Matkov's terse comment when her teenage son, Tom, sat down to a delectable meal that she had spent hours perfecting, and after one bite announced, "Not bad, Mom. Now, this is the kind of stuff Rob's live-in maid cooks every night—only she doesn't make such a mess in the kitchen."

I could sympathize. Back when I began the first of now seven books on historic restaurants, that was the same type of "encouraging" dig my then-teenage daughter Daintry delivered at our table.

What did I do? Because Daintry was a good driver and a photographer, I started taking her with me to the restaurants when school schedules permitted. Little by little, she and her sister, Shannon Heather, began not only to develop an appreciation for unusual and simply prepared food, but to gain a sense of history. As they listened to the stories and saw the quality of craftsmanship in these buildings, they began to understand the importance of preserving them. Listening to the pride of the preservationists, who undertook the research and often spent long hours in tedious, backbreaking work, made an impression on my daughters. This impression was underscored further in our kitchen, where they were called on to stir this or measure that.

Admittedly, the original reason I sought out restaurants in restored buildings was to record their stories. I wanted that kinship with the past. From the beginning, Becky's main interest in the project lay in having the opportunity to spotlight her favorite subject: interesting old buildings being preserved and restored and used in economically viable ways.

We have discovered that our nation's history is unveiled in places that range from the simple and unpretentious to the glamorous and opulent. Yet each building, being a minimum of fifty years old (part of the criteria used for the National Register of Historic Places), has defined our heritage in a multitude of ways. Many of the buildings were private homes whose occupants added interesting footnotes to the daily life of that period. Others have served as a school, a retail store, a hospital, a houseboat—even a rabbit hutch. We've seen the influences of many ethnic regions and celebrate the new foods that have been introduced to our palates.

What I think is important here is not just that Becky and I are cheerleaders for the preservationists or the restaurateurs; the value lies in awakening a comprehension in our society (and our children) that one of the purposes of restoration is to bring the thing that is restored back into the mainstream. And there is nothing more mainstream than the superb food served in the historic restaurants featured here. Add to this the fact that we were able to reproduce their recipes in our kitchens, and our project has a real raison d'être.

The best news to my ears is, as Becky says, "More historic restaurants are opening every day. This is being made possible, in part, by historic preservation tax incentives that encourage developers to rehabilitate, rather than destroy." For us, it also created a pleasant problem: there were far more than fifty eligible restaurants from which to choose. Your favorite restaurant might not have made this printing due to that problem, and for these sins of omission we apologize.

We hope this book helps guide our readers to many pleasant dining experiences in those restaurants that preserve our heritage and give us pride in our past.

CONTENTS

xi

DeFuniak Springs

Fort Walton Beach

Pensacola

Panama City

Apalachicola

Havana

Wakulla Springs

High Springs

Gainesville

Ocala

Cedar Key

Mount Dora
Winter Park
Orlando

Fernandina Beach

St. Augustine

Lakeland

Tampa • Lake Wales

St. Petersburg Beach

Sarasota

Palm Beach

Bokeelia
Captiva Island

Fort Myers

Boca Raton

Lighthouse Point

Fort Lauderdale

Miami Beach
Miami
Coral Gables

Fort Myers Beach

Key West

HOPKINS BOARDING HOUSE
Pensacola

HOPKINS BOARDING HOUSE

Diners from town, and from all over, sit elbow-to-elbow beside the boarders at Hopkins Boarding House in Pensacola. Perfect strangers are soon talking and laughing while mounds of home-cooked vegetables and meats and biscuits are passed around, family-style. On Tuesday, Friday, and Sunday, when the famous Fried Chicken is served, folks line up in droves.

Arkie "Ma" Hopkins opened her boardinghouse in 1948. The spacious two-story frame home, built in 1900, is located in the North Hills historic district and is surrounded by wonderful old rambling houses and tree-filled yards.

Ma Hopkins ran a tight ship. No drinking was ever allowed on the premises, and no smoking, either, and no hats were allowed at the table. When finished, everyone was expected to carry their plates to the kitchen. But her kindheartedness and gracious Southern hospitality made the Hopkins Boarding House a Gulf Coast tradition. One boarder who passed away in 1993 liked it so much he stayed here more than thirty years.

Since her death in December 1986, Ma Hopkins's son, Ed, an attorney, and his wife, Vicki, are continuing to run the boardinghouse in the same tradition. Ed Hopkins recalls childhood memories of his mother staying up all Saturday night cooking pies for Sunday dinner. Though they still serve cakes, cobblers, and puddings, he told me, "Most people today generally have no room left for dessert."

The morning I visited, I was welcomed into the homey, oak-paneled, high-ceilinged dining room, where staff members had just finished snapping green beans for lunch.

In addition to twelve bushels of green beans a week, they serve a vast array of other fresh vegetables—like turnip greens, collards, pole beans, cabbage, carrots, butter beans, squash, okra, and black-eyed peas—along with rice, gravy, and muffins. Chicken and Dumplings, Beef Stew, Roast Beef, Ham, Liver, and Fried Chicken are served on alternating days.

After a tour of the house, I enjoyed a hearty breakfast of an Omelet with grits, sausage, and biscuits while I chatted with a few lingering customers. As I left, I looked longingly at the front porch, where "there's always a breeze," and wished I had time to do what so many diners do—just sit and rock a spell.—B. R. M.

Hopkins Boarding House is located at 900 North Spring Street in Pensacola. Breakfast hours are from 7:00 to 9:30 a.m.; lunch hours are from 11:15 a.m. to 2:00 p.m.; and dinner hours are from 5:15 to 7:00 p.m. The dining room is closed Saturday and Sunday evening and all day Monday. For reservations, call (904) 438-3979.

HOPKINS BOARDING HOUSE'S
STEWED OKRA AND TOMATOES

2 pounds fresh okra
  (or 3 10-ounce packages
  frozen okra)
3 16-ounce cans tomatoes,
  chopped

1 cup chopped onions
¼ cup bacon drippings
salt and pepper to taste

Wash, trim, and slice the okra. Combine all the ingredients. Do not sauté. Simmer on top of stove in a covered saucepan or skillet, or bake in a 350-degree oven in a tightly covered casserole for 30 to 45 minutes. Check okra for desired tenderness. Serves 8 to 10.

HOPKINS BOARDING HOUSE'S
SWEET POTATO SOUFFLE

4 cups mashed sweet potatoes
½ cup sugar
1 stick butter or margarine
½ cup grated coconut
⅓ cup raisins

1 teaspoon lemon extract
  (or orange peel)
1½ cups miniature
  marshmallows

While the potatoes are hot, add all the other ingredients except marshmallows. (If potatoes are dry, add up to ½ cup

3

evaporated milk.) Place in a casserole dish and cover with marshmallows. Bake in a 300-degree oven until the marshmallows are brown, about 20 to 30 minutes. Serves 6.

HOPKINS BOARDING HOUSE'S
CHICKEN AND NOODLES

1 stewing chicken	2 onions, chopped
3 quarts water	1 green pepper, chopped
8 ounces flat egg noodles	½ cup chopped celery
2 cups tomato sauce	2 teaspoons oregano
1 cup tomato paste	salt and pepper to taste

Place chicken in a large pot and cover with water. Simmer until tender, an hour or so. Remove chicken from broth and let cool. Set aside. Cook noodles in the broth until almost tender. Add remaining ingredients; cover and simmer until vegetables are tender, about 30 minutes or so. While the vegetables are cooking, remove the bones from the chicken and cut the meat into bite-size pieces. Return chicken pieces to the pot just before vegetables are done. Heat through and serve. Serves 6.

JAMIE'S FRENCH RESTAURANT
Pensacola

JAMIE'S FRENCH RESTAURANT

The Seville Historic District is an area of gracefully restored eighteenth- and nineteenth-century buildings on the bay in Pensacola. Boutiques, historic churches, the West Florida Museum of History, and the Pensacola Historical Museum draw visitors daily. Art shows, festivals, and Mardi Gras bring in the crowds.

And sitting in the middle of it all is Jamie's French Restaurant. Located in a simple Victorian cottage, Jamie's provides out-of-town visitors with an unanticipated delight and rewards an appreciative regular clientele with continued excellence.

The four-room "shotgun-style" frame structure, with its tin roof and center hall, boasts a front porch complete with a swing. According to owner Gary Serafin, when the house was built in 1860, it was the practice to tax front-yard space; consequently, the lot is small in the front and deep in the rear. Double fireplaces are still the only source of heat in the restaurant. Lace curtains, wallpaper decorated with birds and flowers in tones of burgundy and cream, wooden floors, pink linen tablecloths, and fresh flowers provide a restful, lovely setting for the wonderfully prepared food.

An excellent wine list has won the restaurant numerous awards since 1985. An interesting or unusual wine is listed on the menu under each entrée to encourage diners to complement their meal with a perfect choice.

Jamie's specializes in French cuisine with a Florida flair, with Chef Michael Liebeno using many local and imported ingredients. Specials vary daily, featuring such items as Roast Quail with Shiitake Mushroom and Lump Crabmeat Stuffing, Fresh Snapper with Shrimp and Orange Garlic Chive Hollandaise, and Poulet Roti Au Peche, free-range chicken topped with peach chutney.

The homemade soups are wonderful—whatever the *potage du jour* is, try it!—and the appetizers are such delights as Vol-Au-Vent Avec Escargot—puff pastry filled with a ragout of snails and wild mushrooms.

The last time I was there, as I relished the last bite of my sinfully rich Bailey's Irish Cream Cheesecake, I observed two businessmen engaged in serious conversation at one end of the room. At another table sat a grandmother, a mother, and a little girl dressed in ruffles and bows who was using her most ladylike manners. All were enjoying the fine food and ambiance of this genteel Victorian setting.—B. R. M.

Jamie's French Restaurant is located at 424 Zaragosa Street in Pensacola. Lunch is served from 11:30 a.m. until 2:30 p.m. Tuesday through Saturday. Dinner is served from 6:00 until 10:00 p.m. Monday through Saturday. For reservations (recommended), phone (904) 434-2911.

JAMIE'S FRENCH RESTAURANT'S
BAILEY'S IRISH CREAM CHEESECAKE

2½ pounds cream cheese
1¾ cups sugar
¾ ounce cornstarch
3 ounces Bailey's Irish
  Cream liqueur
¼ ounce vanilla
½ teaspoon salt

4 whole eggs
4 yolks
½ cup heavy cream
¼ cup milk
6 ounces white chocolate
1 prepared graham cracker
  piecrust

Cream cheese with sugar and cornstarch. Scrape the bowl well and add Bailey's, vanilla, and salt. Add eggs and yolks one at a time and incorporate. Put heavy cream, milk, and white chocolate in a small pot and heat gently until chocolate melts; add to cheese mixture. Pour into piecrust. Bake in water bath at 350 degrees for 1½ hours or until set in the center.

JAMIE'S FRENCH RESTAURANT'S
SAUMON FUME LIEBENO

2 tablespoons olive oil
1 small red onion, sliced
3 ounces capers
2 ounces fresh dill, chopped
12 ounces penne or other
  tubular pasta, cooked

9 ounces smoked salmon,
  cut into strips
juice of 2 lemons

In a large pan, heat oil over high heat until almost smoking. Add onion and capers and toss quickly for several seconds. Add dill and pasta and toss for 10 more seconds. Add salmon and lemon juice, rolling the pan to distribute all ingredients evenly. Add salt and pepper to taste. Divide evenly into six small appetizer bowls. Garnish with lemon wheels. Serves 6.

JAMIE'S FRENCH RESTAURANT'S
LONGE DE PORC AU POIVRE VERT

6 pork tenderloins
1 clove garlic, chopped
salt and pepper
⅛ cup black huckleberries
⅛ cup green peppercorns
½ ounce crème de cassis
  liqueur

3 cups veal stock (can
  substitute canned
  beef broth)
1½ cups heavy cream

Rub pork with garlic and season with salt and pepper. Grill the tenderloins. While the pork is cooking, place the huckleberries, peppercorns, and crème de cassis in a saucepan; reduce until almost all the liquid is gone. Add the stock and reduce by half. Add the heavy cream and reduce by half again, or until mixture reaches sauce consistency. Serve sauce warm over sliced pork. Serves 6.

1912 THE RESTAURANT
Pensacola

1912
THE RESTAURANT

The first time I saw the building that is now the Pensacola Grand Hotel was by accident. I was traveling with my family to Alabama, and we took a foray into Pensacola to see the Seville Historic District. "Stop!" I yelled. "I want to see that restored train station."

The lobby of the hotel, with the original hexagonal mosaic tile and ticket windows, was wonderfully done. "Good for them," I said to myself, "and hooray for preservation!"

On my latest trip there, it was a pleasure to see the hotel bustling with conference delegates, enjoying the charm of the past enhanced with modern amenities.

Listed on the National Register of Historic Places, the L & N passenger depot was built of yellow brick in 1912–13 at a cost of $150,000. It served the Pensacola rail industry for fifty-eight years until 1971, when the last train rolled out. After years of disrepair, the depot was purchased by developers, who spent $2 million on the restoration project, completed in June 1984. The French-clay tile roof was removed piece by piece, coded, cleaned, and reinstalled. The ceramic tile floors, the marble baseboards, and the oak stair rails and window casings throughout the building were returned to their original rich luster. A fifteen-story glass addition tucked between the depot and the railroad tracks houses the hotel rooms. In 1993, the current owner, T.B.H. Corporation, spent another $3 million on additional renovations for the Pensacola Grand Hotel.

The restaurant is located in a room added to the terminal in the 1930s to handle baggage storage. Its handsome interior, done in shades of gold and black, is highlighted by brass inlaid mirrors from the first building of Lloyd's of London.

The restaurant is casual for breakfast and lunch, but in the evening, the atmosphere becomes more formal. For dinner, steaks and a wide variety of chicken entrées are offered, with an abundance of seafood specialties such as the delicious Shrimp Maison. Mike Tassen's signature dessert, Strawberries 1912, provides an ambrosially delicious finale to any meal, whatever the entrée.—B. R. M.

1912 the Restaurant is located in the Pensacola Grand Hotel at 200 East Gregory Street in Pensacola. Breakfast is served from 6:30 until 11:00 a.m. Lunch is served from 11:00 a.m. until 4:00 p.m. Dinner is served daily from 6:00 until 10:00 p.m. For reservations, call (904) 433-3336.

1912 THE RESTAURANT'S SHRIMP MAISON

8 large shrimp, peeled and
  deveined
¼ cup white wine
1 tablespoon butter
5 mushrooms, sliced
¼ cup cream

1 teaspoon crushed garlic
1 teaspoon shrimp base
  (optional)
pinch of white pepper
⅓ cup diced tomatoes

Sauté shrimp in wine and butter. Add mushrooms and sauté for about two minutes. Drain off wine and butter. Set aside. In another skillet, add cream, garlic, shrimp base, and white pepper. Boil for 30 seconds. Turn down heat, then add shrimp, mushrooms, and diced tomatoes. Sauté 4 to 6 minutes, until liquid is reduced. Serve over angel hair pasta. Serves 1.

1912 THE RESTAURANT'S
SEAFOOD PONTCHARTRAIN

1 6-ounce fish filet
1 tablespoon white wine
3 tablespoons butter
3 large Gulf shrimp

2 ounces crabmeat
3 tablespoons Béarnaise
  sauce

Broil filet with white wine and 1 tablespoon butter. Sauté shrimp and crabmeat in 2 tablespoons butter for 3 minutes or so and place on top of broiled filet. Top with Béarnaise sauce. Serves 1.

11

STRAWBERRIES 1912

2 tablespoons butter
2 tablespoons brown sugar
2 tablespoons white sugar
juice of ½ fresh orange
juice of ½ fresh lemon
1½ cups sliced fresh
 strawberries

2 ounces Grand Marnier
 liqueur
1 ounce Triple Sec
 liqueur
1½ cups vanilla
 ice cream

Melt butter and add sugars and orange and lemon juice. Reduce over low heat until mixture starts to caramelize. Add strawberries, Grand Marnier, and Triple Sec and continue to caramelize a few minutes more. Pour over vanilla ice cream and serve immediately. Serves 1.

PERRY'S SEAFOOD HOUSE
Pensacola

PERRY'S SEAFOOD HOUSE

The old red house with the Perry's sign on its roof could tell many stories. The stories would begin in 1858, when the Caro family, who paved Pensacola's early streets with brick and ships' ballast, began construction of their two-story frame home. They would continue through the Civil War, when Pensacola was under siege.

The stories would go on to mention the lumber boom years of the 1880s, when a watchman on the second floor searched for ships, then took a lantern and rowboat to pilot them through the sand-laden entrance to Bayou Chico. They would tell of the tollkeeper who ferried passengers across the channel. There would be stories of the well-known Gulf Coast artist Manuel Runyan, who lived here and taught art on the front porch in the 1930s and 1940s. And undoubtedly, there would be tales of the 1950s, when it became a fraternity house for Pensacola Junior College.

For the last twenty years, ever since Perry Baniakis, Sr., opened his restaurant here, the house has been a familiar landmark to Pensacolans as *the* place to eat seafood. A wall of celebrity photos, ranging from June Allison and Bob Hope to John Wayne, Clint Eastwood, and Pernell Roberts, shows it's not just sought out by locals, either.

Though a gazebo-shaped bar with a pegged pine floor is "a little fancier," the main dining area at Perry's boasts a simple décor, with oak floors, the original fireplace, and formica-topped tables. People come to Perry's not for the atmosphere, but for the good seafood—broiled, baked, or fried. Gulf shrimp, scallops, Florida lobster, catfish, and oysters are served with French fries or grits, coleslaw, and hushpuppies.

Perry's was the first restaurant to serve snapper throats. Once, when snapper filets were cut for shipping north, the throats were considered waste and were taken home by the workers to eat. But as soon as Perry's started serving them, the pure white, firm meat from the throat of the Pensacola red snapper became a culinary hit.

And judging from the ones I tasted, I can understand why. Served with Perry's own Tartar and Cocktail sauces, the freshly fried fish was delectable. Another favorite I sampled was the Key Lime Pie, with a three-inch-high meringue. "When one of these pies is carried across the room," I was told, "every lady in the room starts ordering one."

I don't know about *every* lady, but I know this one did.
—B. R. M.

Perry's Seafood House is located at 2140 South Barrancas Avenue in Pensacola. Hours are from 11:00 a.m. until 9:00 p.m. Sunday, Wednesday, and Thursday, and until 10:00 p.m. Friday and Saturday. The restaurant is closed on Monday and Tuesday. Reservations are not accepted. For information, call (904) 434-2995.

PERRY'S SEAFOOD HOUSE'S BAKED FISH

1 to 2 cloves garlic, crushed
1 cup olive oil
juice of 1 lemon

1 8- to 10-ounce grouper
filet
parsley flakes for garnish

Mix garlic, olive oil, and lemon juice. Rub the filet with a little olive oil and bake at 350 to 400 degrees for 15 to 20 minutes, until done. Pour the garlic, olive oil, and lemon mixture over it and sprinkle with parsley flakes. Serves 2.

PERRY'S SEAFOOD HOUSE'S REMOULADE SAUCE

3 cups chopped celery
1 bunch green onions
2 tablespoons dry mustard

½ gallon mayonnaise
6 anchovies, canned

Grind celery and onions into a paste in a meat grinder or food processor. Mix with other ingredients. This sauce is good on boiled shrimp served on a bed of lettuce. Yields approximately ¾ gallon.

PERRY'S SEAFOOD HOUSE'S COCKTAIL SAUCE

2 cups chili sauce
4 tablespoons Worcestershire
   sauce
2 cups ketchup
2 teaspoons dry mustard

2 teaspoons salt
4 tablespoons horseradish
   (creamed)
3 teaspoons black pepper
juice of 1 lemon

Mix all the ingredients together and serve with oysters, scallops, shrimp, or other boiled or fried seafood. Store in the refrigerator. Yields approximately 5 cups.

SCOTTO'S RISTORANTE ITALIANO
Pensacola

SCOTTO'S
RISTORANTE ITALIANO

In 1752, Spanish colonists established Pensacola as a permanent settlement near present-day Seville Square. Today, this area is a lively center of restoration work, with many eighteenth- and nineteenth-century cottages and mansions being turned into shops and galleries. The heart of the Seville Historic District is Seville Square, a public park used for festivals, art shows, and other special events.

Overlooking this square is Scotto's Ristorante Italiano, located in a charming one-story house built in the 1880s. The rose frame building, with a hip roof, is accented with white gingerbread trim on the front porch and cream shutters. For many years, the structure was the home of the Jazz Musicians Union.

The restaurant is owned by Richard Scotto and his wife, Pat. Family portraits of the Scotto family are spotlighted on the walls. One is of Genaro and Lucia shortly after their arrival from Italy's Isle of Capri. Another is of Richard's father, "Pappa Joe," in the 1920s; this picture became the basis for the restaurant's logo.

The Scotto men have always been the cooks in the family, founding the Premier Bakery in Pensacola in 1945. Grandfather Genaro taught son Guiseppe treasured family recipes, and now grandson Richard carries on the tradition as he prepares classic—and exceptional—Italian masterpieces.

To Pat Scotto fell the task of decorating the restaurant, which she did in soothing colors of pink and green, applying stenciling to the walls herself. She also manages up front and has the pleasant job of being official taste tester.

This is a duty I envy after my sampling of some of their delectable dishes. The menu selections feature everything from Fettucine Scotto, made with crabmeat and shrimp, to Veal Marsala and Chicken Cacciatora. They make their own pasta daily, and all ingredients are fresh.

The Ravioli with Italian Sausage, served with a tangy tomato sauce, was delicious, as was the Red Fettucine. I also tried the Stuffed Eggplant with Crabmeat, and it was fabulous. "Richard's Famous Homemade Cheesecake" lived up to its reputation. And my own reputation as a cook wasn't harmed a bit when I tried Richard's recipe out at home.

Just add their authentic Italian music to their Italian food, and you have a romantic evening worthy of the Riviera.
—B. R. M.

Scotto's Ristorante Italiano is located at 300 South Alcaniz Street in Pensacola. Lunch is served from 11:30 a.m. until 2:00 p.m. Monday through Friday. Dinner is served from 5:30 until 10:00 p.m. Monday through Saturday. For reservations (recommended), call (904) 434-1932.

SCOTTO'S RISTORANTE ITALIANO'S STUFFED EGGPLANT WITH CRABMEAT

4 medium-size eggplants	1 cup seasoned
3 celery stalks, diced	breadcrumbs
1 onion, chopped	½ cup Parmesan cheese
1 red bell pepper, diced	6 ounces cooked shrimp
2 teaspoons fresh garlic,	6 ounces fresh lump
chopped	crabmeat
2 tablespoons butter	1 teaspoon salt
4 ounces olive oil	1 teaspoon black pepper

Remove stems from eggplants and split them oblong. Place eggplants in boiling water for 2 minutes, then put them in ice water. Scrape the meat from the eggplants and reserve skin. Sauté celery, onions, peppers, and garlic in butter until soft. Mix with eggplant meat, olive oil, breadcrumbs, Parmesan cheese, shrimp, crabmeat, and seasonings; combine well. Put this stuffing back in the eggplant skins and bake at 325 degrees for 20 minutes, until golden brown. Serves 4.

SCOTTO'S RISTORANTE ITALIANO'S "RICHARD'S FAMOUS HOMEMADE CHEESECAKE"

Crust:
1 cup graham cracker crumbs   3 tablespoons sugar
3 tablespoons melted butter

Combine the ingredients and press into the bottom of a 9-inch springform pan.

Filling:
1½ pounds cream cheese   2 cups sour cream
¾ cup sugar   1 teaspoon vanilla
3 eggs

When the cream cheese is at room temperature, combine it with the sugar in a mixer; cream the cheese with sugar until smooth. Add eggs one at a time, beating well after each addition. Add sour cream and vanilla. Pour batter into crust and bake for 1 hour and 15 minutes at 300 degrees. Turn oven off and leave cheesecake in oven for 2 hours. Yields 1 cheesecake.

STAFF'S
Fort Walton Beach

STAFF'S **W**omen should wear a color that goes well with pink when they come to Staff's for dinner during the winter camellia season. Octogenarian twin sisters Agnes and Frances pass out their home-grown flowers along with cakes and candies they make each day for the restaurant's desserts. Their father, Theodore Staff, built the Gulfview Hotel (behind Staff's) in 1913 and at one time served three meals a day.

In 1931, when Theo Bass married Agnes Staff, he began developing the restaurant into what you see today. This family-oriented restaurant displays not only the swimming medals and trophies of the twin sisters and their siblings, but snapshots of children whose descendants continue to make their annual pilgrimage to Staff's. Now on the National Register of Historic Places, Staff's has the distinction of being Florida's oldest seafood restaurant.

Old favorites like Shrimp Cocktail head the appetizer list, but the new, Western-influenced Crabmeat-Stuffed Green Chilies topped with cheese and Staff's Quesadilla are giving hefty competition. Even though folks flirt with the trendy dishes, they generally end up ordering the traditional Onion Rings, just one of Staff's specialties.

It's not only seafood that Staff's knows how to make. The marinated Stir-Fry Chicken with Vegetables is a favorite among landlubbers. And speaking of vegetables, the tangy Cold German Potato Salad is such a standout that I'll never make it any other way than by their recipe. Steaks are on the menu, too, and I'm told they are almost as popular as the seafood.

The price of Staff's child's plate hasn't changed in over twenty years, because they want to encourage families to bring their children. What children usually appreciate most is the restaurant's variety of desserts; what parents appreciate is that desserts are included in the price of all meals. Children can't resist the fresh, homemade Chocolate Peanut Logs and Pecan Candy concoctions, and adults have a difficult time choosing among the Blueberry and Black Forest cheesecakes, Sister Frances' Angel Food and Divinity Cake, and Pineapple Upside-Down Cake. It's simply decisions, delicious decisions at a restaurant that tugs at your heart with its caring charm.

Staff's is located at 24 Miracle Strip (U.S. 98) in Fort Walton Beach. Dinner is served from 5:00 until 9:00 p.m. Sunday through Thursday and from 5:00 until 10:00 p.m. Friday and Saturday. The restaurant is closed Thanksgiving and Christmas. Reservations are not necessary. For information, call (904) 243-3482.

STAFF'S COLD GERMAN POTATO SALAD

4 to 6 baked potatoes
4 to 6 scallions including
  stems, chopped
1 red or green pepper,
  chopped

garlic salt to taste
⅓ to ½ cup commercial
  Italian dressing

Peel and cube potatoes and put in a medium bowl. Add scallions, peppers, garlic salt, and Italian dressing. Mix ingredients and adjust seasoning as needed. Serves 6.

STAFF'S SISTER FRANCES'
ANGEL FOOD AND DIVINITY CAKE

Angel Food Cake:
1 cup sifted cake flour
1½ cups sugar
¼ teaspoon salt
12 egg whites

1¼ teaspoons cream
  of tartar
1 teaspoon vanilla extract
¼ teaspoon almond extract

Sift flour with ¾ cup of sugar and salt 4 times. Beat the egg whites with cream of tartar and extracts until soft peaks form. Add remaining sugar carefully, about 2 tablespoons at a time, beating well after each addition. Sift ¼ cup of the flour mixture over egg whites and fold in carefully, then fold in the remaining flour mixture a little at a time. Pour mixture into a greased and floured 9-by-12-inch pan and bake in a preheated 375-degree oven for 35 to 40 minutes, until cake tests done in center. Invert cake pan onto a rectangular plate and let cool. Tap sides of pan and lift from cake. When completely cool, slice cake lengthwise into 2 layers.

Chocolate frosting:

½ cup butter, softened
4 cups confectioners' sugar
3 squares unsweetened
  chocolate, melted
2 egg yolks
2 teaspoons vanilla

⅓ cup half-and-half or
  heavy cream
2 to 3 tablespoons strong
  coffee
½ cup broken pecans

In a mixer, cream butter and ½ cup of sugar. Add chocolate. Add egg yolks one at a time, beating after each addition. Add vanilla and beat thoroughly. Gradually add remaining sugar and cream as needed to allow mixture to become thin enough to spread. Spread thin on all layers of cake, because a layer of divinity will cover chocolate layers. Take remaining frosting and add coffee until frosting reaches a runny consistency. Reserve remaining frosting and pecans.

Divinity:

2 egg whites
1½ cups sugar
1½ teaspoons light
  corn syrup
5 tablespoons
  cold water

pinch of cream of
  tartar
1½ teaspoons vanilla
  extract

Combine all ingredients except vanilla in top of a double boiler over very hot, but not boiling, water. Blend well. Place over rapidly boiling water and beat constantly with electric mixer for 6 to 7 minutes. Don't overcook. Remove from heat and stir in vanilla with electric mixer for about 2 minutes. Let cool. Spread divinity over chocolate frosting, assembling layers. Spread divinity on all sides of cake. Stir reserved runny chocolate frosting and pour mixture over cake, letting it run down the sides. Sprinkle pecans over the top. Yields 1 cake.

BUSY BEE CAFE
DeFuniak Springs

BUSY BEE CAFE

The reason this luncheon restaurant isn't called "Fried Green Tomatoes," after its signature Fried Green Tomato Sandwich, is to honor DeFuniak Springs' original Busy Bee Restaurant. A 1916 photograph shows the first Busy Bee, located in a building across the street. Retired University of Mississippi professor-owners Drs. Dennis and Brenda Ray have resurrected the spirit and some of the recipes of the first Busy Bee, though they have relocated the restaurant to the Brown Green Building at the back of their soon-to-be antique mall.

Many restored buildings recycled into restaurants have walls decorated with all manner of antique bric-a-brac. It's attractive and nostalgic and gives guests a nice, warm feeling. But the Rays are purists, and their focus on restoration is different. They only use antiques that are functional or that might have decorated a restaurant's walls in 1910, when their building was constructed. For instance, a handsome 1893 furnace heats the dining room. And opposite the simple oil-cloth-covered table where I sat was a still-operating 1923 General Electric refrigerator that has never been repaired! (My waitress removed a couple of lemons from it for my lemonade.)

As I ordered lunch, a guest cranked up the Regina Victrola. Unless you've heard music from one of these old crank Victrolas, it's difficult to describe the clarity of its melodious tones. Those pure tones were interrupted by the ringing of a hand-cranked telephone. Brenda Ray confided that business associates frequently telephone their employees here, because guests get such a kick out of talking on the old black telephone.

On the chilly winter day that I visited, I tried two of their special soups. The hearty Navy Bean with Ham has a taste I couldn't identify until the secret came out. The dry beans aren't soaked, but rather cooked with all the spices from the beginning. This allows a more flavorful taste to be cooked right into the bean.

But the Busy Bee's *pièce de résistance* is its Fried Green Tomato Sandwich. Dipping the tomatoes in cornmeal and grilling them allows the juices to squeeze through the crusty cornmeal for a crunchy, juicy taste. Then add the taste of bacon and you're courting a new cliché. Instead of folks saying something is like "bacon and eggs," they'll say it's like "bacon and fried green tomatoes." (Well, maybe not.)

The restaurant has only one dessert on its menu and needs only one. That's how good it is. Leave space for the creamiest Peanut Butter Pie that you have ever tasted.

Collectors of an amazing number of antiques—four hundred clocks among them—the Rays take interested guests through a restaurant side door to an adjacent hallway of antique appliances. These and the Rays' knowledge will entertain and amaze you. Shelves of four-sided toasters and outdated but still-functioning pieces are on display. These will become part of this antique mall that should be in operation by the time you read this book.

Closing out the lunch hour, Dennis Ray showed me one of his favorites—an 1890 Star Vacuum Cleaner. He demonstrated by pumping the vacuum cleaner like an accordion to operate it. One hundred–plus years later, it's still being used every day and getting the job done, and even more phenomenally, with a man operating it.

The Busy Bee Cafe is located at 2 North Seventh Street in DeFuniak Springs. Lunch is served from 10:30 a.m. until 1:30 p.m. Monday through Saturday. For reservations, call (904) 892-6700.

BUSY BEE CAFE'S
NAVY BEAN WITH HAM SOUP

2 tablespoons shortening
1 cup yellow onions,
  chopped
1 cup smoked ham
5 quarts water
1 pound dry navy beans
1 tablespoon parsley flakes

1 clove garlic, minced
1½ teaspoons salt
1 teaspoon pepper
¼ teaspoon or more Tabasco
  sauce
¼ teaspoon ground nutmeg

In a soup pot, melt shortening over high heat. Add onions

27

and ham and sauté until onions are light brown. Add water and bring to a boil. Add dry beans and remaining ingredients. Return water to a boil, reduce heat, and cook uncovered at a slow, rolling boil for approximately 3 hours, until beans are tender and soup thickens slightly. Stir frequently. (It is not recommended that dry beans be presoaked. Dry beans will thus absorb the full flavor of the ingredients.) To serve, top with fresh chopped onions accompanied by cornbread. Yields 5 quarts.

BUSY BEE CAFE'S
FRIED GREEN TOMATO SANDWICH

1 cup cornmeal, ground fine
1 tablespoon flour
½ teaspoon salt
¼ teaspoon ground
　black pepper
½ teaspoon garlic powder
3 medium green tomatoes,
　sliced
½ cup milk

1 tablespoon cooking oil
　or butter
4 teaspoons or more butter
4 6-inch Po-Boy buns
　(hoagies)
8 teaspoons mayonnaise
8 slices bacon, fried and
　drained

In a small, shallow bowl, combine cornmeal, flour, salt, pepper, and garlic powder. Dip sliced green tomatoes in milk and coat with meal mixture. Spread oil or butter evenly on grill or in a cast-iron skillet and fry green tomatoes until golden brown on both sides. Spread about ½ teaspoon of butter lightly inside each half of each bun; spread mayonnaise over butter to cover as desired. Place 2 slices of bacon on the bottom half of each bun. Cover with 4 slices of fried green tomatoes and top half of bun. Serves 4.

MIA'S CAFE
DeFuniak Springs

MIA'S CAFE

By looking, you wouldn't know that the stylish building that now houses Mia's Cafe and Gift Shop was built in 1905. Today's fancy awning and interior atrium don't display the building's double-thick brick walls or its age. But dated photographs show that the building, built by Knox Gillis for his law office, occupied this location at that date.

Knox was a proud DeFuniak Springs citizen who appreciated the tiny town that the Chautauqua Movement chose for its summer home in 1885. The Chautauqua Movement, a strong religious, educational, and entertainment movement, was the town's moving force for many years. Remnants of its glory are evident in the 1886 library, where you'll find an amazing collection of weapons and artifacts dating back to the Crusades. On summer Chautauqua weekends, four thousand visitors would come to town to learn and be entertained at the grand, white brick Chautauqua Building. You can still see this building silhouetted in one of the world's only two completely circular natural lakes. Victorian homes line this lovely lake. Visitors can even peddle beside it on the DeFuniak Springs Welcome Center's surrey-topped, four-wheeled, side-by-side bicycle built for two.

After a morning outing around the lake, I wheeled over to Mia's Cafe for lunch. The Country French–style restaurant is on the building's second floor, wrapped around a wide atrium that overlooks Mia's Victorian-influenced gift shop, which is as enticing as the peach-and-green restaurant décor. Some of the gift shop's more decorative items can be seen nestling on window ledges and various pieces of furniture scattered throughout the dining rooms.

A library table holds racks of imported and domestic wines, including those from the local Chautauqua winery—a whimsical oxymoron, since the movement strictly forbade alcohol.

At Mia's, French Apple or Orange and Sour Cream muffins are the first item set upon each peach-colored linen tablecloth. Fresh flowers at each table provide an attractive accent. Here, you can dine as lightly or heartily as you please. A fruit-based Chicken Salad will please those who want something a bit different from standard chicken salad. Between light and crispy is the Chicken Stir-Fry, which gains in popularity each time it appears on the menu. However, Mia's hallmark dish is the earnestly hearty Zucchini Vegetable Pie. A great accompaniment to the pie is a glass of Chautauqua Vineyards Nobel, a fruity red with a rich bouquet. Mia's offers a variety of old-time cobblers and popular desserts, but the ones you don't want to pass by are the Coconut Cream and Lemon Cream pies.

Mia's Cafe is located at 24 Baldwin Avenue in DeFuniak Springs. Lunch is served from 11:00 a.m. until 3:30 p.m. Monday through Saturday. Reservations are not necessary. For information, call (904) 892-MIAS.

MIA'S CAFE'S ZUCCHINI VEGETABLE PIE

Crust:
Prepare 1 piecrust to fit a 10-inch pie plate, or use a commercial product. Bake the piecrust according to recipe or package directions and set aside.

Filling:
2 tablespoons olive oil	4 cloves garlic, minced
2 tablespoons margarine	½ cup cabbage, shredded
2 medium zucchini, chopped	salt and pepper to taste
2 medium yellow longneck squash, chopped	½ cup mayonnaise
1 cup fresh mushrooms, sliced	1 cup mozzarella cheese, shredded
1 small to medium onion, chopped fine	2 to 3 dashes Worcestershire sauce
2 medium carrots, sliced diagonally	2 dashes Tabasco sauce
½ cup green bell pepper, chopped fine	2 medium tomatoes, sliced thin

In a large cast-iron skillet, melt and blend oil and margarine over medium-high heat. Add next eight ingredients a little at a time and sauté slightly, leaving vegetables crunchy. Add salt and pepper and remove from skillet. Drain thoroughly through a strainer. Combine mayonnaise, half of cheese, Worcestershire, and Tabasco and stir until well mixed. Add drained vegetables to mayonnaise mixture and stir until thoroughly incorporated. Place sliced tomatoes over entire bottom of prebaked pie shell and spoon in vegetable mixture, distributing evenly. Top with remaining cheese, place in a preheated 350-degree oven, and bake for 45 to 60 minutes. Serves 6 to 8.

MIA'S CAFE'S CHICKEN STIR-FRY

1 tablespoon sesame oil
3 tablespoons margarine
   or butter
1 large green pepper,
   julienned
1 medium onion, julienned
1½ cups uncooked chicken
   breast, coarsely chopped
4 large fresh mushrooms,
   sliced

1 tablespoon minced garlic
1 teaspoon Mei Yen
   seasoning (Spice Islands)
1 tablespoon red pimiento,
   chopped
¼ cup teriyaki sauce
2 to 3 servings of rice
   cooked according to
   package directions

Melt and blend oil and margarine in a cast-iron skillet or wok on high heat. Add green pepper, onions, and chicken and sauté until chicken begins to lose pink color. Add mushrooms, garlic, and Mei Yen and reduce heat to simmer, stirring continually. When skillet is simmering, add pimiento and teriyaki sauce, stirring to incorporate. Cook only to season through. Serve over rice. Serves 2 to 3.

THE GREENHOUSE RESTAURANT
AND LOUNGE
Panama City

THE GREENHOUSE RESTAURANT AND LOUNGE

An area in the Greenhouse Restaurant's downstairs dining room reminds me of a European mews. A narrow brick path runs beside a rough-plastered wall where stained-glass window insets are interspersed with scrub oak trees. The opposite wall features flower-filled window boxes beneath windows reminiscent of a clapboard cottage. The mews area exudes a romantic atmosphere that would have been difficult to imagine in 1927, when the building was erected for the *Panama City News Herald*.

Restaurateur Mike Mahowald built floor-to-ceiling windows throughout the entire wall of his downstairs dining room. To achieve his surreal greenhouse, he has planted a large garden lanai of exotic trees and has strategically lit certain trees with tiny white lights.

Whether you're a downtown businessperson or not, you're bound to receive a "power lunch" either here or in the more casual upstairs dining room. If you're trying to stay on the light side, the Chicken and Shrimp Almond Salad performs a great marriage between meats from opposing backgrounds. And for that matter, the Char-Grilled Chicken Teriyaki comes in well below the 350-calorie count. The Greenhouse offers pastas, sandwiches, and soups that stand up well to the Heart Association's checklist.

The soup to try is the Spicy Tomato, which made me glad that Thomas Jefferson introduced the tomato to America. Quiche Lorraine is always popular, but be sure to ask about their Quiche du Jour. The cool and drizzly day that I visited, the Southwest-inspired Sausage and Black Beans was a surprising success.

As I munched on the thick and chewy Caribbean Bread with Sunflower Seeds, I tried to decide which of the dinner entrées to choose. I gave in and tried a kind of unusual surf and turf. The Washington Culinary Institute–trained Mahowald does a special seasoning that doubles for both entrées. My Grouper Meunière had a delicious lemon-based sauce, while the sweet vermouth and cream sauce of my Filet Maison was nothing short of sensational.

Another reason this restaurant brings people back down-town for dinner is the desserts. They are prepared by Mahowald's seventy-six-year-old mother-in-law, Marie Fluharty, who also arranges the restaurant's flowers and paints still lifes that hang in the upstairs dining room. Her Chocolate Eclair Cake gets the most votes, but Chocolate Almond Crunch Pie and Blueberry Delight are both so deli-cately sweet and creamy that they slip down too fast.

The Greenhouse Restaurant is located at 443 Grace Avenue in Panama City. Lunch is served from 11:00 a.m. until 2:00 p.m. Monday through Saturday and dinner from 5:00 until 10:00 p.m. Monday through Saturday. For reservations (ac-cepted), call (904) 763-2245.

THE GREENHOUSE RESTAURANT'S FILET MAISON

Seasoning Mixture:

4 tablespoons salt	1 tablespoon thyme
1 tablespoon pepper	1 tablespoon oregano
1 tablespoon garlic powder	1 tablespoon basil

Place ingredients in a jar and shake until thoroughly mixed.

4 8-ounce filets mignons	1 cup fresh mushrooms,
Seasoning Mixture	sliced
(recipe above)	½ cup sweet vermouth
3 tablespoons olive oil	1 pint heavy cream

Season filets on both sides with Seasoning Mixture. Heat olive oil in a cast-iron skillet on medium-high until almost smoking. Place filets in skillet and sear heavily on both sides until a nice crust forms. Remove filets and keep warm. Add mushrooms and a pinch of the seasoning mixture to the skil-let. Cook for 1 minute, stirring continually. Add vermouth and reduce volume to half of original amount. Add cream, lower heat, and reduce to half of volume again. While sauce is reducing, broil filets to desired doneness. When both sauce

35

and filets are ready, place each filet on a warmed plate and ladle equal amounts of sauce over each. Serves 4.

THE GREENHOUSE RESTAURANT'S
GROUPER MEUNIERE

Seasoning Mixture
  (see previous recipe)
2 9-ounce grouper filets
flour for dusting
3 tablespoons olive oil

juice of l lemon
⅓ cup white wine
3 tablespoons very cold
  butter

Sprinkle Seasoning Mixture over flesh side of fish and dust lightly with flour; shake off excess. Heat olive oil in a cast-iron skillet on medium-high. Place filets in skillet with flesh side down. Cook until a brownish crust forms; turn and add lemon juice and wine. Stir liquid mixture and cook filets for about 2 minutes. Remove filets from skillet. Add butter to skillet, stirring to dissolve. Return filets to skillet to flavor through. Serve filets on warmed plates and pour remaining sauce over top. Serves 2.

THE GIBSON INN
Apalachicola

THE GIBSON INN

The peppy sounds of ragtime music from the Gibson Inn's old piano had my toes tapping even before I entered the dining room. The music makes it hard to think formal in a fancy dining room where brass and green-glass-shaded lamps bathe the pine walls. Although many of the inn's heart-pine floors have been replaced or covered with a green Victorian-pattern carpet, the inn's yesteryear attitude makes you wish you'd planned for a longer stay. And that's before you've even tasted the food.

At the turn of the century, guests chose to stay at James Fulton "Jeff" Buck's relaxing inn for fresh oysters and seafood cooked any way they wanted. Guests continue to come to the comfortable inn for the same reasons. Oh, you can still get the full oyster repertoire, but let me suggest that you try the inn's new oyster trademark, Oysters Remick. The blend of Swiss cheese, chili sauce, and horseradish that tops each oyster cuts right through the usual strong oyster taste, yet preserves the distinctive flavor that has made this region famous. If you've come for lunch, the Oyster Stew is as popular here as clam chowder is in Boston. However, if Soft-Shell Clams are in season, go for the recipe that sautés them with garlic.

You can get good veal and steak here, but I figure this close to the ocean, I'm not going to squander a chance to have Shrimp, Scallop, and Crab Dijon. The chef's Dijon Butter is the secret ingredient. It enhances this light but flavorful seafood ensemble that is placed upon whispery-thin puff pastry. I also sampled the Grouper Rockefeller, an obvious spin on oysters Rockefeller; the addition of smoked ham gives this dish a richer, more flavorful succulence.

For dessert at the Gibson Inn, it takes a will power of undiluted grit to pass up the tangy Key Lime Pie. This velvety, tart pie tasted as if the limes had been picked that morning. And chocoholics who love pecan pie loaded with pecans will love the Chocolate Bourbon Pecan Pie.

Neither in 1907, when the inn was built, nor in 1923, when it was sold to the Gibson sisters, Annie and Sunshine, would the owners have served international coffees—especially not the current Gibson Specialty, made with rum, Kahlúa, triple sec, and about a teaspoon of coffee. All I can say of this wonderful concoction is that I was glad I only had to climb the stairs to my third floor bedroom. It was fabulous.

The Gibson Inn is located at 51 C Avenue (U.S. 98) in Apalachicola. Breakfast is served from 7:00 until 10:30 a.m. and lunch from 11:30 a.m. until 2:00 p.m. daily. Dinner is served from 6:00 until 9:00 p.m. Monday through Thursday and from 6:00 until 10:00 p.m. Friday and Saturday. For reservations, call (904) 653-2191.

THE GIBSON INN'S
SHRIMP, SCALLOP, AND CRAB DIJON

¼ cup butter
3 shallots, sliced
1 pound shrimp, peeled, split, and cleaned
1 pound scallops
8 or 9 fresh mushrooms, sliced
¼ pound crabmeat
¼ cup white wine
salt and pepper to taste

8 4-inch puff pastry shells (homemade or commercial), baked
8 slices provolone cheese
3⅛-inch slices Dijon Butter per serving (recipe follows)
8 lemon wedges
parsley for garnish

Melt butter in a large skillet on medium-high. Add shallots and sauté lightly; add shrimp and scallops, sautéing until almost done. Lower heat to medium; add mushrooms, crabmeat, white wine, salt, and pepper. Stir until flavors are combined and seafood is done. Place puff pastry shells in cassoulets, then place on a baking sheet. With a slotted spoon, divide equal amounts of seafood mixture into pastry-lined dishes and top each with a slice of cheese and 3⅛-inch slices of Dijon Butter. Bake in a 500-degree oven for 5 minutes, until puff pastries are golden brown. Garnish with lemon wedges and chopped parsley. Serves 8.

39

Dijon Butter:
¼ pound butter, softened   ½ cup breadcrumbs
¼ pound margarine, softened   ¼ cup Worcestershire sauce
½ teaspoon garlic   ⅛ cup A-1 sauce
¼ cup parsley

Combine all ingredients in mixing bowl and beat on low speed for 1 minute, then beat on high speed for 10 minutes. Divide into parchment paper or heavy wrapping paper and freeze for later use. Yields about 1 pound.

THE GIBSON INN'S OYSTERS REMICK

⅓ cup mayonnaise   1 dozen Apalachicola
3 teaspoons chili sauce   oysters
1 level teaspoon horseradish   2 slices Swiss cheese, grated

Combine mayonnaise, chili sauce, and horseradish; set aside. Place each opened and drained raw oyster on half of its shell, then place on a baking sheet. Top each equally with mayonnaise mixture and shredded cheese. Bake in a preheated 500-degree oven for 5 minutes, until cheese melts, or place oysters under the broiler for 2 to 3 minutes. Serves 2 to 4.

WAKULLA SPRINGS LODGE
AND CONFERENCE CENTER
Wakulla Springs

WAKULLA SPRINGS LODGE AND CONFERENCE CENTER

I am torn. Part of me wants to let you know about this "nature lover's paradise," where you really can get away from it all, and the other part wants to keep it a secret. The springs here are so ancient that the same mastodon bones seen by Ponce de Leon in 1513 can still be seen at the bottom of the 185-foot-deep crystal-clear springs. The Indians called the place Wakulla, "Mysteries of Strange Waters." Ponce de Leon believed it was the fountain of youth. When neither he nor his crew grew any younger, Ponce de Leon left, disillusioned. Six years later, feeling that he had been hasty, he returned to the springs but found hostile Indians. They fought in a battle that subsequently resulted in the explorer's death.

Soon after entering the 1937 lodge built by Edward Ball, I realized that this is a place to relax and take off your watch. The lobby is dominated by a great stone fireplace, and its cypress ceiling is decorated with murals hand-painted by a German craftsman believed to have once served Kaiser Wilhelm. Crossing the rose-and-beige marble floors, I went to my room, which had spindle beds, its original Persian rug, and a great view of the dock.

Within minutes, I was at that dock preparing to board their jungle cruise. Live alligators swam beside us, and we photographed hundreds of unusual birds and other wildlife before switching to a glass-bottomed boat. This boat allowed us to watch tropical fish thread through the natural underwater cliffs in this crystal-clear spring, which flows at an incredible rate of six hundred thousand gallons a minute.

The cruise certainly worked up my appetite, so I headed straight for the dining room upon docking. It's hard to put a name to the dining room's décor. The white-and-rose table linens, old-fashioned rose-patterned china, and black-leather rocking chairs make you think of a more comfortable time. The cuisine itself conjured up a Southern plantation which belied the décor. I ordered the Stuffed Cornish Hen Supreme with Wild Rice, very tender and moist with a yummy stuffing. My collaborator, Becky, told me not to leave without getting the Blueberry Sour Cream Pie, so I sampled both that

42

and the Key Lime Pie. The Key Lime was delicious, and the marriage of tart blueberries with sour cream and whipped cream was an ideal union.

For any getaway, this lodge and four-thousand-acre wildlife sanctuary offer a one-of-a-kind experience that I suppose I shouldn't keep to myself.

Wakulla Springs Lodge and Conference Center is located fifteen miles south of Tallahassee on Highway 61 South in the Edward Ball Wakulla Springs State Park. Breakfast is served from 7:30 until 10:00 a.m.; lunch is served from noon until 2:00 p.m.; and dinner is served from 6:00 until 8:30 p.m., daily. For reservations, call (904) 224-5950.

WAKULLA SPRINGS LODGE'S STUFFED CORNISH HENS SUPREME WITH WILD RICE

4 1½-pound Cornish hens
1¼ cups chopped scallions
1 cup chopped mushrooms
2 tablespoons butter
2 cups soft breadcrumbs
1 hard-boiled egg, chopped
¼ cup sour cream
¼ teaspoon garlic salt
⅛ teaspoon pepper
¾ cup milk
½ cup water
1 envelope chicken gravy
  mix (commercial)
2 dashes ground nutmeg
1 4-ounce package wild rice,
  cooked

Rinse hens and pat them dry. Cook 1 cup of the scallions and ½ cup of the mushrooms in butter until they are tender and the liquid evaporates. Combine with breadcrumbs, egg, sour cream, garlic salt, and pepper. Lightly stuff hens with this mixture; truss. Place hens breast side up in a large, shallow baking pan. Cover with foil and roast in a 350-degree oven for 1 hour. Uncover; baste with drippings, spooning off and saving 2 tablespoons of drippings. Return hens to oven and roast 30 to 40 minutes, until tender and browned. Sauté remaining scallions and mushrooms in reserved drippings in a small saucepan. Stir in milk, water, gravy mix, and nutmeg; bring to a boil, stirring. Simmer 1 minute. Serve hens with this sauce on a bed of wild rice. Serves 4.

WAKULLA SPRINGS LODGE'S
NAVY BEAN SOUP

1 pound dried navy beans
5 cups water
1 10-ounce can beef
  consommé
1 chicken bouillon cube
4 potatoes, diced

2 onions, diced
4 tablespoons butter
4 carrots, diced
2 cups chopped ham
3 bay leaves
salt and pepper to taste

Soak beans overnight in enough water to cover them. Rinse and place navy beans, water, consommé, and bouillon cube in a large pot. Bring to a boil, then cover and simmer for 2 hours. Add potatoes to soup pot. Sauté onions in butter until partially cooked. Add to soup pot along with remaining ingredients. Simmer, covered, for 1 hour, until vegetables are done. Serves 6 to 8.

WAKULLA SPRINGS LODGE'S
BLUEBERRY SOUR CREAM PIE

1 cup sugar
½ teaspoon salt
¼ cup all-purpose flour
2 eggs
2 cups sour cream

¾ teaspoon vanilla
1 9-inch graham cracker
  pie shell, unbaked
1 can blueberry pie filling
1 cup whipped cream

In a mixing bowl, combine the first 6 ingredients and mix well. Pour into the pie shell and bake in a preheated 350-degree oven for 30 minutes, until the center is set. Top hot pie with blueberry filling. Chill several hours. When ready to serve, top with whipped cream. Yields 1 pie.

NICHOLSON FARMHOUSE RESTAURANT
Havana

NICHOLSON FARMHOUSE RESTAURANT

Secluded at the end of a bumpy dirt road stands the plantation home that Dr. Malcolm Nicholson built in 1828. Anytime you come, the setting is a scenic mist of nostalgia, not unlike an old sepia photograph. But every May when the Lord rolls out a yellow carpet of "dye flowers" in the home's front pasture, that old photo turns into a sunshine-colored vision of how meadows and pastures used to look.

Dr. Nicholson semiretired from medicine when he moved to Havana, Florida, from Fayetteville, North Carolina, to become a corn and cotton planter. His ideas on construction were quite original for the time. He used weatherboard for the home's exterior, believing that brick interiors provided better insulation. The bricks were handmade on the site, which is why you'll see animal paw prints and a child's hand print—thought to be one of his children's—preserved on a brick wall in one of the front dining rooms opposite the fireplace. Original, never-varnished pine doors remain throughout the home. Cut from pines on the four-thousand-acre plantation, they show wavy ridges due to being smoothed by hand with a drawing knife. Be sure to look up at the hand-hewn ceiling beams still held in place by pegs.

I dined in a former toolshed attached to the front porch. Descendant Paul Nicholson told me that in earlier times, the shed was left open for itinerant preachers to use when traveling through the area late at night. When built, the shed didn't open into the main house, but its interior wall was removed when the home was renovated in 1987. Today, its wallpapered walls display decorative wreaths and farm implements that look as if they've just been brought in from the field.

It's best to have a farmer's appetite when you visit this family-run restaurant, because dinner here won't let you go away hungry. No alcohol is served, but a carafe of iced tea (sweetened or not) is set upon your checked tablecloth, accompanied by a big bowl of Southern Boiled Peanuts. They're unique—soft yet crunchy. Try not to keep popping these addictive morsels into your mouth. And don't be tempted to eat too much of the Caribbean Bread with chewy sunflower seeds or the homemade Yeast Rolls before the main course.

Though the menu lists Fish, Pork Chops, Chicken, and even a Vegetarian Platter (ordered in advance), the entrée to order here is Steak, with maybe a side order of Herbed Broiled Shrimp or Sautéed Mushrooms and Onions. Paul Nicholson told me that they cut their own meat, then age and season it. And though you can request steak sauce, none is needed for any of their six cuts of beef, ranging from Porterhouse to Tenderloin. My Filet Mignon oozed with tender flavor, and I requested their Twice-Baked Potato recipe, which they would have shared with me, except that they were unsure of ingredient amounts. "Oh, we just keep adding to it until it tastes good," was the cook's reply. The "addings" are cheddar cheese, sour cream, chives, and garlic.

Save room for dessert, because Mama Ann (Paul's better half) makes a light and luscious Banana Split Cake that offers a lilt to your savory meal.

Nicholson Farmhouse Restaurant is located three and a half miles west of Havana on State Road 12. Dinner is served from 4:00 until 10:00 p.m. Tuesday through Saturday. For reservations, call (904) 539-5931.

NICHOLSON FARMHOUSE RESTAURANT'S SOUTHERN BOILED PEANUTS

3 quarts dried Spanish   **½ cup salt**
  red-skinned peanuts   **water**

Place peanuts in a large stock pot. Add salt. Add enough water to cover peanuts. The pot should be a little over ¾ full. Place a lid on the pot and bring to a boil. Cook for 2½ hours, checking occasionally and adding *hot* water as needed to keep peanuts covered. Turn heat off and let sit for 1 hour. Taste for saltiness. If peanuts are not salty enough, add more salt to water and let stand; taste frequently until they reach desired saltiness. If they are too salty, pour off salt water, replace it with clear water, and let stand; taste frequently until they reach the desired saltiness. Dip out and allow to cool, or eat warm. Do not cook peanuts until soft or they will lose flavor. Yields 3 quarts.

NICHOLSON FARMHOUSE RESTAURANT'S BANANA SPLIT CAKE

Crust:

1 stick margarine, melted   **½ cup sugar**
2 cups graham cracker crumbs

In a medium bowl, combine margarine, graham cracker crumbs, and sugar until evenly mixed. Spray a 9-by-12-by-2-inch pan with nonstick coating and distribute crumb mixture over bottom and up sides of pan, pressing firmly into place. Place in a preheated 350-degree oven and cook for 6 minutes. Remove and let cool.

Filling:

2 sticks margarine, softened   **1 15-ounce can crushed**
1-pound box confectioners'   **pineapple**
   sugar   **½ cup pecans, crumbled**
2 large eggs   **1 8-ounce container**
½ teaspoon vanilla extract   **whipped topping**
2 large bananas, sliced   **maraschino cherries**

Cream margarine with an electric mixer and add sugar a little at a time until creamy. Add eggs one at a time, mixing about 2 minutes each, until well incorporated. Continue beating on high speed until light and fluffy. Add vanilla and mix until blended. Spoon filling evenly into cooled crust. Place sliced bananas in tight rows over filling, covering entirely. Drain pineapple and spread evenly over bananas. Sprinkle pecans evenly over pineapple. Smooth whipped topping over filling and refrigerate for at least 6 hours. Place 1 maraschino cherry in the center of each piece. Yields 9 generous pieces.

THE PALACE SALOON
Fernandina Beach

THE PALACE SALOON

I'm told that teetotalers come to the Palace Saloon just to drink in the atmosphere. The heavy red-velvet draperies admit a bare slice of sunlight, giving the room a feeling of intimacy. Patrons appreciate the hand-carved mahogany caryatids supporting the mirror over the forty-foot bar and the old, polished oak tables and mosaic tile floor. When you come to the Palace Saloon, you feel as if you've stepped into a very fancy saloon in an old Western movie.

In 1878, Josiah H. Prescott, who served as a Union lieutenant during the occupation of Fernandina in the Civil War, returned here to begin his haberdashery and shoe business. Before erecting his Renaissance Revival building, Prescott anchored the foundation in six feet of crushed oyster shells. It was not until 1903 that German-born Louis G. Hirth turned the structure into a saloon. Old advertisements announced that the saloon offered Red Cross Rye, Turkey Mountain Corn Whiskey, and Cognac Bouchée Frères. Hirth was obviously of a literary bent, for in 1907 he hired Roy Kennard to paint the literary murals that hang above the marble wainscoting.

Back in those days, before ladies frequented saloons, the story goes that a local woman was showing her visiting friend around town one day on horseback. Her daring friend wanted to see the inside of the Palace Saloon, so she and her hostess rode their horses right through the swinging doors and up to the bar. The bartender, not to be outdone, promptly poured a beer for one of the horses, which the thirsty animal reportedly drank in one gulp!

For a short while during Prohibition, the Palace served as an ice-cream parlor, but it has continued as a bar ever since, and now it serves lunch.

The first thing I learned while touring the premises is that this is the kind of place where you can't remain a stranger for very long. The regulars insisted that I try the infamous twenty-two-ounce Pirates Punch. I'm not sure what was in this pungent fruit-based drink except rum and gin, but I do know that more than one is bound to end your workday. Never able to resist Onion Rings and Peel-'n-Eat Shrimp, I had a feast and was rewarded with their recipes. The regulars insisted that I sample bites of their lunches, too.

The Palace Saloon is the kind of place where, if you have not "let go" before entering, you certainly will before leaving.

The Palace Saloon is located at 117 Centre Street in Fernandina Beach. Meals are served from 11:00 a.m. until midnight Monday through Saturday and from noon until 11:00 p.m. on Sunday. Reservations are not necessary. For information, call (904) 261-6320.

THE PALACE SALOON'S PEEL-'N-EAT SHRIMP

1 medium onion, sliced
1 lemon, sliced
2 tablespoons seafood
 seasoning

1 teaspoon cayenne pepper
1 pound shrimp with shells
2 to 4 tablespoons salt

Fill a 4-quart pot about half full of water. Place onion, lemon, seafood seasoning, and cayenne pepper in pot and bring to a boil. Add shrimp. As soon as the water boils again, turn off heat. Let stand about 5 minutes. Add salt 1 tablespoon at a time and taste every couple of minutes until salty to taste. Drain and serve. Serves 2.

Note: For spicier shrimp, add a few dashes of Tabasco sauce.

THE PALACE SALOON'S ONION RINGS

2 to 3 large Spanish onions
2 eggs
2 cups buttermilk

6 ounces beer
1½ to 2 cups vegetable oil
2 cups all-purpose flour

Peel skin from onions and cut onions diagonally into thick slices. Separate rings and set aside. In a deep bowl, beat eggs and add buttermilk and beer, mixing until well combined.

Heat oil in an electric frying pan to 350 degrees, or in a small saucepan until very hot, but not smoking. Moisten onion rings in milk mixture, then place in flour, making sure rings are covered. Remove from flour and dip back into milk mixture and again into flour. When you have prepared enough rings to fill the frying pan, place them carefully into the hot oil. Cook until golden brown. Repeat the process until all rings are fried. Serves 4 to 6.

Note: A liberal sprinkling of Creole seasoning will add extra spice.

LE PAVILLON
St. Augustine

LE PAVILLON

The owners of Le Pavillon were taken aback when a chauffeur-driven limousine pulled up one day and an armed bodyguard came in to check the place out, followed by actress Brooke Shields and her mother, who had come for lunch. Like numerous other celebrities, they had made a special trip to St. Augustine to taste the culinary wonders of Le Pavillon.

Since 1977, when Chef Claude Sinatsch and his German-born wife, Giselle, opened their restaurant in a charming old home on San Marco Avenue, Le Pavillon has won a wide reputation for its Continental cuisine. Small wonder, since Claude was trained in Switzerland at the hotel his family owned, the Sports Hotel in Davos. He later worked as a chef at internationally renowned hotels in Europe and Bermuda before deciding to join his brother-in-law in St. Augustine.

"We always liked Florida," he told me, "and we fell in love with the European style of St. Augustine."

The family lives in the upstairs of the spacious house they purchased for Le Pavillon. The original structure was built before the turn of the century as a five-room cottage. Located in the Abbott Tract along what was once Route 1, it was a popular tourist home for many years, with vacationers returning season after season. Additions were built by every new owner, including the Sinatsches, who added a room in front to enlarge their seating area.

The interior of the restaurant, decorated by Giselle, is warm and mellow, with stained glass, lace curtains, a mantel and fireplace, and antique glassware in curio cabinets. The bar is framed by the beautifully carved pineapple posts of a century-old bed.

Everyone in the family works at the restaurant. Claude cooks, Giselle works "up front," her brother, Fritz Dold, is the maître d', daughter Patricia serves, and teenage son Claude helps "when he's not out surfing."

The night I was there, it was raining outside, and the Sinatsches made me feel very much like I was a guest in their cozy home.

Le Pavillon is well known for its crêpes and veal. "And

some say our Rack of Lamb is the best in the country," volunteered Giselle. Seasonal specialties such as Quail, Venison, and Goulash are also offered. But nothing could have been better than the "Claude's Bouillabaisse" they served me—succulent pieces of fresh seafood, perfectly seasoned, exquisitely presented, and accompanied by freshly made Rolls with Herb Butter and a glass of excellent German wine. It was pure bliss!—B. R. M.

Le Pavillon is located at 45 San Marco Avenue in St. Augustine. Lunch is served from 11:30 a.m. until 2:30 p.m. and dinner from 5:00 until 10:00 p.m. every day. For reservations (recommended for weekends), call (904) 824-6202.

LE PAVILLON'S POULET AU FROMAGE

1 8-ounce boneless
  chicken breast
1 mushroom, diced
1 small shallot, diced
1½ tablespoons sherry wine
¼ teaspoon parsley,
  chopped fine
salt and freshly ground pepper
  to taste

2 thin slices Swiss cheese
2 pats butter
2 thin slices mozzarella
  cheese
breading
oil for deep-frying

Flatten the chicken breast with a mallet and set it aside. Sauté mushrooms and shallots for several minutes, then add sherry and parsley. Cook until most of the liquid has evaporated. Remove from heat. Lay out flattened breast and season with salt and pepper. Top with Swiss cheese, the mushroom mixture, butter pats, and mozzarella. Fold the breast in half. Bread the chicken and deep-fry it in oil, then bake it in the oven at 450 degrees for 10 to 15 minutes (or flour it and sauté in butter until lightly browned, then add in stock with a dash of sherry until done). May be served with a poulette, supreme, or madeira sauce. Serves 1.

LE PAVILLON'S "CLAUDE'S BOUILLABAISSE"

2 pounds seafood (lobster,
fresh mussels, clams,
haddock, turbot or brill,
whiting, eel, and crabmeat)
2 large onions, chopped
3 cloves garlic, crushed
2 tomatoes, chopped
½ cup oil
sprig of thyme, chopped

sprig of fennel, chopped
bay leaf
pinch of fresh saffron
salt and pepper to taste
strip of orange peel
4 cups boiling water
4 to 6 slices French bread
sprig of parsley, chopped
4 to 6 pats herb butter

Cut the fish into 2-inch lengths; keep the coarse and the more delicate fish on separate plates. Put the onions, garlic, and tomatoes in a saucepan with the oil, herbs, seasonings, and orange peel. Add the coarser varieties of fish, cover with boiling water, and cook for 5 minutes on a very quick fire. Put in the remaining fish and continue boiling another 5 minutes (10 minutes hard boiling altogether). Remove from heat. Strain the liquid into soup plates on slices of French bread. Arrange fish on top. Sprinkle with parsley and top with a dab of herb butter. Serves 4 to 6.

Note: The object of this very fast boiling is to blend the oil and water thoroughly. Cooked slower, the oil would not mix properly and would rise to the surface. And if the fish is cooked any longer, it will break and spoil in appearance and flavor.

RAINTREE RESTAURANT
St. Augustine

RAINTREE RESTAURANT

Like much earlier English settlers, the MacDonald family sailed across the Atlantic to America in hopes of realizing their dreams and ambitions in the New World. They sold most of their belongings and began their voyage on March 30, 1979, in a forty-five-foot yacht. They stopped at the Canaries, then Barbados, before reaching St. Augustine, which they had liked on an earlier visit.

Once settled in St. Augustine, the enterprising MacDonalds bought and renovated the Victorian house at 102 San Marco Avenue, turning it into a stunningly beautiful restaurant.

The house was built in 1879 by Bernard Masters, a Confederate veteran who provided houses for each of his five daughters. It became the residence of daughter Hattie after her marriage to A. J. Collins, who was in the dry-goods business. After World War II, the house was converted into the Corner House restaurant, well known for its Southern cooking.

The MacDonalds have added a glassed-in room to the front porch and a lovely, landscaped brick courtyard at the side entrance to the restaurant. Along the courtyard and brick path is an outdoor aviary full of beautiful small birds and an attractive Japanese pond. The inside rooms have been decorated with exquisite wallpaper and authentic antiques. The 1650 Jacobean cradle and the 1415 chair in the hallway are family pieces of the MacDonalds.

As in many historic restaurants, the entire family is involved in running the business, with a goal of giving St. Augustine diners "fine food in beautiful surroundings." Their numerous culinary awards attest to their continuing success. Tristan MacDonald pointed out the temperature controlled wine room that displays more than 4000 bottles of wine. "*Wine Spectator* magazine rated us as having one of the 250 outstanding wine lists in the world," he said with pride.

Raintree offers diners a wealth of options. Entrées range from Brandy Pepper Steak and Champagne Chicken, to Bourbon Street Lobster and Blackened Yellowfin Tuna.

"We have an outstanding dessert chef," Tristan told me,

and from a sampling of the sinfully rich pastry cart, I knew he was right.—B. R. M.

Raintree Restaurant is located at 102 San Marco Avenue in St. Augustine. Dinner is served daily from 5:00 until 9:30 p.m. For reservations (recommended on weekdays and necessary on weekends), call (904) 824-7211.

RAINTREE RESTAURANT'S SEA SCALLOPS IN TOMATO AND YELLOW PEPPER VINAIGRETTE

2 ounces peanut oil
1½ cups flour
1 teaspoon salt
½ teaspoon pepper
2 pounds large sea scallops
1 cup tomato, seeded and
   diced
½ cup yellow bell pepper,
   diced
2 ounces (by volume)
   basil, chopped

2 ounces (by volume)
   chives, chopped
½ cup white wine
½ cup fish stock (clam
   juice may be substituted)
2 teaspoons balsamic
   vinegar
linguini, cooked

Heat oil in a large, heavy skillet on medium-high. Season flour with salt and pepper, mixing well. Dredge scallops in flour and place in skillet; sauté on both sides until golden brown. Remove scallops with a slotted spoon and let dry on a paper towel. Add tomatoes, bell peppers, basil, and chives to the skillet and sauté for 1 to 2 minutes, until vegetables are barely soft but still retain their color. Add wine and fish stock; reduce volume by half. Add vinegar and taste; add salt and pepper if desired. Return scallops to skillet and heat through. Serve scallops and sauce over linguini. Serves 4.

Note: If clam juice is used, salt may not be needed.

RAINTREE RESTAURANT'S ROASTED PECAN MERINGUE WITH RASPBERRIES AND FRESH CREAM

8 egg whites
1-pound box confectioners' sugar, sifted
2 tablespoons cornstarch
1 teaspoon red wine vinegar

1 cup roasted pecans, chopped
1 pint fresh raspberries, strawberries, or kiwi
mint leaves for garnish

Beat egg whites in an electric mixer at medium speed until foamy; gradually add sugar and cornstarch and beat at high speed until egg whites form peaks and become stiff, but not dry. Beat in vinegar. With a hand whip, fold in pecans very slowly, being careful not to flatten egg whites. The meringue should be firm and opaque.

Cut 2 8-by-11-inch pieces of wax paper to fit into 2 jelly-roll pans. Lightly oil wax paper. Divide meringue in half and spread each half onto a jelly-roll pan. Bake in a preheated 275-degree oven until meringue is a light brown color, about 50 minutes. Let cool (but not in refrigerator). Reserve fresh fruit and mint leaves.

Chantilly Cream:
1 pint heavy whipping cream
1 tablespoon granulated sugar
1 teaspoon vanilla extract

Whip cream in an electric mixer until stiff. Add sugar a teaspoon at a time. Add vanilla and mix until combined. Let sit in the refrigerator a few minutes. Transfer cream into a piping bag or use a spoon when ready to ice both layers.

To assemble, remove wax paper from bottom of meringues. Place first meringue on platter and pipe or spoon half of Chantilly Cream over meringue; add second layer of meringue and pipe remaining cream over top. Garnish with fresh raspberries and mint leaves. Slice meringues to preferred size. Yields 12 squares.

SANTA MARIA
St. Augustine

SANTA MARIA

For years, throngs of hungry customers have flocked to the Santa Maria restaurant on the pier in St. Augustine to enjoy eating the seafood on their plates—and to enjoy feeding the fish in the water below.

Ever since the 1950s, when the present owner's father, Louis S. Connell, started feeding fish daily from his restaurant, thousands of mullet, catfish, trout, and sea bass have begged for their supper. As the fish jump and splash, the human diners watch and open trapdoors at their tables to oblige the fish with tidbits.

The Santa Maria is as nautical an atmosphere as you could want. Not only is the restaurant surrounded by water, with beautiful views of moored sailboats, but the décor itself features fishnets and ropes and ships' lanterns and wheels.

In 1763, shortly before Spain lost Florida to Great Britain, Spaniards built the first pier on Matanzas Bay on the site where the Santa Maria stands today. In the 1860s, Civil War soldiers enjoyed the pier while recuperating at an adjacent hospital. Following a fire in 1885, the pier was rebuilt, complete with a building that served as a house, then as a fish market, and finally, following World War II, as a restaurant.

Hurricane Dora tore up much of the eastern side of the restaurant in 1964, though as much as possible of the original structure was saved. Current owners Carl and Sylvia Connell proudly showed me the 1885 slatted wood ceiling in the bar, the original three-inch-thick heart-pine floors, and their collection of historic photographs.

The Connells are always expanding, it seems, to make room for the crowds that frequent the restaurant during "the season"—from February, when the Daytona 500 is held, through Labor Day. "We've done a project a year," Sylvia told me. "We're adding a porch now."

Though steak, chicken, and spaghetti are served for diehard landlubbers, the Santa Maria specializes in Broiled Flounder and a Seafood Platter with fried shrimp, oysters, deviled crab, scallops, clams, and fish. A children's menu is also offered.

I couldn't resist sampling their satisfying Black Bean Soup, which the Connells often are asked to bring to community gatherings. The Shrimp Creole—made from Sylvia's own recipe—was spicy and wonderful. And oh, those Hushpuppies. They are uniquely sweet and good. The secret, Sylvia says, is to beat them well: "All that air beaten in makes them light."

The Santa Maria is very much a family-run restaurant with a friendly atmosphere in which people of all ages feel welcome. My only problem was what to leave to feed the fish.—B. R. M.

The Santa Maria is located on the pier at 135 Avenida Menendez in St. Augustine. The restaurant's hours vary with the season, so call ahead. No reservations are accepted. For information, call (904) 829-6578.

SANTA MARIA'S BLACK BEAN SOUP

1 12-ounce bag dry black beans	5 bay leaves
2 cloves garlic, chopped	½ cup cumin
1 medium onion, chopped fine	1 tablespoon thyme
1 medium bell pepper, chopped fine	½ cup red wine vinegar
½ cup olive oil	salt and pepper to taste
2 small ham hocks	6 to 8 cups cooked rice
	½ cup chopped scallions for garnish

Soak beans overnight. Do not drain. When you're ready to cook the beans, add more water, enough to measure 3 inches over the top of the beans. Cook on medium-high heat. Sauté garlic, onions, and bell peppers in olive oil; add to beans along with other ingredients except vinegar, salt, and pepper. Cook for about 2½ hours, until tender. Add vinegar, salt, and pepper and cook another 30 minutes. Put 1 cup of the cooked beans in a blender and purée; add to beans and cook 15 more minutes, until beans thicken. Serve over rice and top with scallions. Serves 8.

SANTA MARIA'S SHRIMP CREOLE

4 16-ounce cans tomatoes
1 large onion, coarsely
  chopped
1 large bell pepper, coarsely
  chopped
4 stalks celery, coarsely
  chopped
1 cup olive oil
6 bay leaves
2 cloves garlic, chopped
1 tablespoon thyme

1 tablespoon oregano
⅓ cup gumbo filé
salt and pepper to taste
¼ cup cornstarch
2 tablespoons water
1½ pounds fresh medium
  shrimp, peeled and
  deveined
4 sticks butter or margarine
4 cups cooked rice

Cook tomatoes over medium heat. Meanwhile, in a sauté pan, sauté onions, bell peppers, and celery in olive oil; add to tomatoes. Add all other ingredients except cornstarch, butter, shrimp, and rice. Cook 2 hours on medium heat. Add cornstarch to enough water to dissolve it, then pour into tomato mixture. Cook an additional 30 minutes, stirring occasionally. Sauté shrimp in butter until tender, then add both shrimp and butter to tomato mixture. Cook 5 more minutes. Serve over rice. Serves 8 to 10.

SANTA MARIA'S HUSHPUPPIES

2 cups self-rising flour
1 cup cornmeal
1 large onion, chopped fine
½ cup sugar

1 tablespoon salt
1 tablespoon pepper
½ to 1 cup water
deep fat for frying

Mix the first 6 ingredients together. Add water, leaving mixture thick enough to dip from a teaspoon. Beat well with an electric mixer, making sure to beat long enough to make the dough light and air-filled. Drop like dumplings into enough hot grease to cover them. Fry until brown. Serves 12.

THE GREAT OUTDOORS
TRADING COMPANY AND CAFE
High Springs

THE GREAT OUTDOORS TRADING COMPANY AND CAFE

In the tiny town of High Springs, just northwest of Gainesville, there is a small cafe where some very innovative food is being served.

Rob and Leslie Justis, formerly canoe outfitters on the Withlacoochee River, opened their Great Outdoors Trading Company in a brick two-story building on the main block of town. Constructed as an opera house in 1895 and 1896, when the town was booming from the railroad and phosphate mining, the building was the hub of the community for years. Stage performances, silent films, and dances drew crowds to the second floor, and a mercantile store sold all sorts of goods on the first floor.

The Justises restored the original heart-pine floors, removed the stucco to expose the brick walls, and proceeded to sell camping equipment and apparel. When the attached one-story building, constructed as a barbershop in 1915, became available, they put a door through the wall, renovated, and expanded into the restaurant business.

The Justises are committed to serving natural, unadulterated food that not only tastes good but is good for you. They don't have a deep-fat fryer on the premises. Everything they prepare is fresh; they refuse to purchase even frozen chickens. Their biscuits are made using only whole-wheat flour. A vegetarian special is offered at every meal, along with their regular menu. Blessedly, no smoking is permitted.

But this is not just a health-food restaurant. The menu contains a wide variety of broiled seafood, interesting soups and salads, fresh vegetables, chicken dishes, and desserts like Hazelnut Torte and Chocolate Mousse. Their cholesterol-free tofu dishes, such as Tofu Florentine and the Sizzler sandwich, have won over the tastes of even die-hard meat-and-potato eaters.

When I was there for Sunday brunch, I enjoyed their Clam Chowder and a tofu Ocean Delight Omelet, filled with shrimp, scallops, and cheddar cheese.

It's easy to understand why visitors who come from every state in the union and many European countries for canoeing, fishing, and the best cave diving in the world have signed the guest register here. The friendly small-town atmosphere, the mellow old building, and the wholesome good food make the Great Outdoors a great place to be.—B. R. M.

The Great Outdoors Trading Company and Cafe is located at 65-85 North Main Street in High Springs. Hours are from 10:00 a.m. until 9:00 p.m. Sunday through Thursday, and until 10:00 p.m. Friday and Saturday. For reservations (recommended), phone (904) 454-2900.

THE GREAT OUTDOORS CAFE'S
JAMAICAN CHICKEN NOUVELLE

1 large shrimp
½ boneless chicken breast
Spike seasoning to taste
black pepper to taste

2 tomato slices
¼ avocado, sliced thin
¼ cup hollandaise sauce

Poach the shrimp and split it lengthwise; set aside. Pound chicken with a mallet until very thin. Broil chicken breast, topped with Spike and pepper. When it is nearly done, remove chicken from broiler and top with tomato slices, avocado slices, and shrimp. Place in a 450-degree oven for 1 to 2 minutes. Top with hollandaise sauce. Serves 1.

THE GREAT OUTDOORS CAFE'S
TOFU SALAD DRESSING

½ cup apple cider vinegar
½ cup tamari (natural
  soy sauce)
1½ cups vegetable oil

½ teaspoon fresh basil
1 pound fresh tofu
2 cloves garlic
¼ cup chopped onion

Mix all the ingredients in a blender until puréed. Serve over salads. Yields 3½ to 4 cups.

THE GREAT OUTDOORS CAFE'S
CLAM CHOWDER

1 large onion, chopped
1 tablespoon butter
½ ounce Spike seasoning
¼ teaspoon black pepper,
  freshly ground
¼ teaspoon Tabasco sauce
¼ teaspoon ground rosemary
⅛ teaspoon celery salt
½ teaspoon thyme

1 baked potato
1 pint heavy cream
1 pint half-and-half
1 baked potato, cubed
1 pound clams, chopped
2 tablespoons finely
  chopped parsley
2 ounces cooking sherry

Sauté onions in butter until transparent. Add seasonings. Mash the baked potato and blend it with cream and half-and-half. Add to the onion mixture and stir well. Add the potato cubes and clams to the chowder and heat over low heat until thoroughly cooked. (Clams should be almost rubbery.) Adjust seasonings to taste and add parsley and sherry. Serves 6.

THE SOVEREIGN RESTAURANT
Gainesville

THE SOVEREIGN RESTAURANT

One hundred years ago, blacksmiths were shoeing horses in the livery stable which is now the Sovereign Restaurant. Built in 1879 as an adjunct to the opera house next door, the yellow brick building changed with the times. It served as a warehouse, a machine shop, and a garage before being converted into the inviting restaurant it is today.

Located near the restored town square of Gainesville and the Hippodrome State Theater, the Sovereign fits well into its surroundings. A handsome iron gate opens from the street to allow diners to enter the restaurant via a brick alleyway that hints of New Orleans. The interior is highlighted by a lovely cathedral ceiling, stained glass, rich wood, and paisley tablecloths. An enclosed patio with original brick floors features Victorian antiques, including a marble-topped shoeshine stand.

Elmo Moser, born in the Swiss Alps and trained as an executive chef, has been running the Sovereign for years. His menu offerings range from Beef Wellington, Saltimbocca, and Chicken Jerusalem to Red Snapper Meunière, with daily specials. On Wednesdays, his wife, Lupe, prepares Mexican dishes, which he says are "always very authentic and always very popular."

Moser encouraged me to try his Scallone à la Sovereign, an entrée of abalone and scallops sautéed with mushrooms. He told me his is one of the few restaurants on the East Coast to serve this, since the abalone must be flown in from California. After tasting this specialty, I could understand the pride he takes in it.

I also enjoyed tasting his Beef Cayenne, with its spicy sauce of cream and cayenne pepper, though it is definitely for those who like it hot. But no matter. The Margarita Pie, made from Lupe's secret recipe, brought soothing relief. No amount of cajolery could induce them to reveal the recipe, but that just gives me one more excuse to visit again.—B. R. M.

The Sovereign Restaurant is located at 12 Southeast Second Avenue in Gainesville. Dinner is served from 5:30 until

70

10:00 p.m. Monday through Thursday and from 5:30 until 11:00 p.m. Friday and Saturday. The restaurant is closed Sunday. For reservations (recommended), call (904) 378-6307.

THE SOVEREIGN RESTAURANT'S SHRIMP ANDERSON

20 ounces frozen leaf spinach, thawed
2 tablespoons butter
garlic salt to taste
salt and pepper to taste
24 large shrimp, peeled and deveined
4 shallots, chopped
juice of half a lemon or more

splash of white wine
8 black olives, pitted and sliced
8 green olives, pitted and sliced
4 ounces Swiss cheese, grated
4 ounces blue cheese, grated

Sauté the spinach with butter, garlic salt, salt, and pepper. Place in an au gratin platter and keep warm. In a second skillet, sauté the shrimp with salt, pepper, butter, and shallots until lightly done. Add lemon juice and white wine. Place sautéed shrimp on top of spinach, sprinkle with olives and mixed cheeses, and bake in a 375-degree oven for 5 minutes. Serve hot with rice or boiled potatoes. Serves 4.

THE SOVEREIGN RESTAURANT'S BEEF CAYENNE

24 ounces sliced beef tenderloin
salt to taste
1 to 2 teaspoons cayenne pepper

½ cup flour
¼ cup white wine
1 cup heavy cream
4 ounces sliced almonds

Put sliced tenderloin on a plate and lightly dust with salt, cayenne pepper, and flour. Sauté in a hot skillet until medium rare. Sprinkle the beef with white wine, then add heavy cream and almonds and bring to a boil. Serve immediately with rice or noodles. Serves 4.

THE SOVEREIGN RESTAURANT'S BROWNIE PIE

3 ounces semisweet chocolate
  morsels
8 ounces sugar
2 whole eggs
1 egg yolk
3½ ounces butter, softened
dash of vanilla

2 ounces all-purpose flour,
  sifted
½ cup heavy cream
1 cup graham cracker
  crumbs

In a double boiler, slowly melt chocolate morsels over low heat. In a mixing bowl, add sugar, eggs, egg yolk, softened butter, and vanilla. Whip until fluffy. Fold in melted chocolate, flour, and heavy cream and stir to incorporate. Butter a 9-inch pie pan and sprinkle it with graham cracker crumbs. Fill with brownie mixture. Bake for 30 minutes at 325 degrees. Yields 1 pie.

THE ISLAND HOTEL
Cedar Key

THE ISLAND HOTEL

Today, you won't find alligator and rattlesnake skins or quinine at this former general store. Those items plus a "restaurant and furnished rooms" were offered here in 1859. That was when business partners Major John Parsons and Francis E. Hale had the structure built with eleven-inch-thick tabby walls. Since that era, it has housed both Confederate and Union troops and withstood such natural and unnatural disasters as a 1896 hurricane and tidal wave, the decline of the cedar lumber industry, and a rumored reputation as a house of ill repute. Possibly worst of all, it has survived having its historic Neptune Bar turned into a coffee and juice bar!

A little of each encounter has shaped the hotel's atmosphere. Its floors slope every way but level. The hotel now contracts and expands with the seasons, with all the aches and pains of an elderly lady. Yet when current owners Tom and Alison Sanders rediscovered the inn in 1992, they gave up their glamorous jobs in international television and marketing research to revive this fading gem.

The Sanderses have completely refurbished the hotel and rebuilt the Neptune Bar—including a restoration of Helen Took's famous Neptune mural—but they have retained the inn's cozy eccentricities. Don't worry, the restaurant still has its famous Hearts of Palm Salad and Potato and Scallion Soup. And if you are like me, you'll have to fight temptation not to fill up on the hot homemade Poppy Seed Bread.

The new owners place emphasis on local foods. Their expanded menu includes Cedar Key Little Neck Clams Florentine, Grouper in Paper, and Oysters, Soft-Shell Blue Crabs, and Stone Crabs in season. If you want a change from seafood, they have Filet Mignon, Rosemary Baked Lamb, and many great vegetarian dishes inspired by the previous owner.

During the spring and fall, the enchanting courtyard is turned into a beer garden, with live Florida folk music. But since the days that balladeer Jimmy Buffett frequented the bar, bringing his Margaritaville attitude with him, I can't think of ordering anything but a Margarita here. You can sip it outside on the hotel balcony as the sun slips below the horizon. This is when you're apt to agree with a former owner who described the place as "an oasis out of the fast lane."

The Island Hotel is located at Second and B streets in Cedar Key. Breakfast is served daily from 8:00 until 10:00 a.m.; dinner is served Wednesday through Monday from 6:00 until 10:00 p.m. The restaurant is closed Tuesday. For reservations (recommended), call (904) 543-5111.

THE ISLAND HOTEL'S GROUPER IN PAPER

8- to 12-ounce fresh
  grouper filet
1 tablespoon olive oil
½ teaspoon Spike seasoning
1 teaspoon fennel seed
½ teaspoon white pepper

½ teaspoon thyme
4 lemon slices, cut
  diagonally
brown rice, cooked
  according to package
  directions

Cut enough parchment paper to completely enclose fish. Rub olive oil over filet and place fish on one-half of parchment paper. Sprinkle Spike seasoning, fennel seed, white pepper, and thyme over fish and place lemon slices equally over top. Fold paper around fish to seal securely. Bake in a preheated 350-degree oven for 15 to 20 minutes. Serve immediately with extra lemon wedges and brown rice. Serves 2.

THE ISLAND HOTEL'S POTATO SCALLION SOUP

2 quarts chicken or
  vegetable stock,
  homemade or commercial
5 pounds new potatoes
2 to 3 tablespoons butter
3 bunches of scallions,
  coarsely chopped

4 cloves garlic, chopped
  fine
2 tablespoons fresh dill
1 pint half-and-half
  (optional)
salt and pepper to taste
raw scallions for garnish

Place stock in a large stock pot on medium-high. Wash potatoes, scrubbing if necessary, and add to stock. Cook until potatoes are tender, about 30 minutes. Remove pot from stove and let cool. In a sauté pan, melt butter on medium-high heat and sauté scallions and garlic. Remove pan from stove and let cool. Process potatoes with stock, scallions, and garlic in a food processor until smooth and creamy. Add dill and process for a few seconds. Pour mixture back into stock pot and heat slowly on medium-low heat. Do not allow to boil. Half-and-half may be added if desired. Season with salt and pepper. Serve with additional raw scallions, julienned or sliced diagonally. Serves 8.

FISH ISLAND HOTEL

1 4- to 8-ounce fresh fish filet or fish steak (shark, grouper, drum, or other nonoily, light fish)

1 tablespoon chopped fresh herbs (thyme, parsley, basil, or dill)

¼ teaspoon Spike seasoning

¼ cup sesame seeds, toasted

¼ cup white wine

4 tablespoons clarified butter

Place fish in a Pyrex pan. Sprinkle with fresh herbs and Spike. Cover almost completely with sesame seeds. Mix the wine and butter and pour over the fish, covering the bottom of the pan no more than ¼ inch deep. Bake at 350 degrees for 10 to 15 minutes, until the fish is light and puffy. Do not microwave. Serves 1.

SPEAKER'S CORNER
Ocala

SPEAKER'S CORNER

To be free to say what's on your mind without fear of backlash is important the world over, a point indelibly punctuated by the establishment of Speaker's Corner at the Marble Arch corner of Hyde Park in London, England. Evelin Lopez, owner of Speaker's Corner in Ocala, Florida, formerly known as First and Broadway, wanted to establish her own kind of restaurant, where people would feel free and relaxed—a casual place where customers could say what was on their minds and where men would feel free to shuck their ties and jackets.

The 1885 three-story Marion Block Building, with its high ceilings and satin-etched windows, looked like the kind of restaurant Lopez could turn into a nurturing place. Lopez did not want a bar atmosphere, although guests are free to prop their elbows on the marble counter of her rich burgundy-and-brass bar and have one of the three European draft beers, a glass of sparkling fruit-flavored water, or a glass of wine. The idea is to come in and relax for a little while in this former opera house and drugstore. Hexagonal tiles from the old drugstore remain intact at the restaurant's entrance. You can also see the original hardwood floors, exposed brick walls, and wainscoting. But the walls are now filled with paintings by local artists.

Lopez got the idea for the restaurant when she came to Ocala to visit her fiancé and found there was no nice place to get a cappuccino and dessert. Now, business people can have lunch inside the restaurant or outside in the Sidewalk Cafe, which overlooks the fountain and palm trees of the town square. And if they want to take something special back to the office or home, they'll have a hard time making a selection at the two European-style deli counters inside the front door. You can select from a variety of desserts and such exotic and wonderful-tasting things as Arabica Beans, Hummus, Tabouli, Spinach Pie, and Terro Chips (from a tropical root). These are also served as appetizers at lunch and dinner.

With so many choices, it's tough to know what to order. The menu changes monthly, and there are always specials at an extraordinarily reasonable price. A great lunch is a bowl of Evelin's Roasted Garlic and Broccoli Soup with her High Roller Sandwich and herbal tea. The special bread is flown in from California and then loaded with a ton of delicious meats and cheese and rolled up like a jelly roll.

For dinner, the list is just as long. You can choose from Grilled Duck Breast with Cherry Sauce, Roast Quail, and Veal Marsala. Let me suggest that you try Evelin's Pâté with Truffles, along with the Terro Chips for an appetizer, the house salad with Shallot Balsamic Vinaigrette, and Pecan Dolphin for your entrée. Then top this off with a piece of Almond Sponge Cake and a cup of espresso or cappuccino.

Such a meal could very well make you a regular at this cozy restaurant.

Speaker's Corner is located at the corner of First and Southeast Broadway in Ocala. Hours are from 11:00 a.m. until 10:00 p.m. Monday through Thursday and until 11:00 p.m. Friday. Saturday hours are from 5:00 until 11:00 p.m. Sunday brunch is served from 11:00 a.m. until 3:00 p.m. For reservations (not required), phone (904) 622-2131.

SPEAKER'S CORNER'S PECAN DOLPHIN

2 8-ounce dolphin filets
¾ cup all-purpose flour
1 teaspoon salt
½ teaspoon white pepper
3 tablespoons clarified butter
1 clove garlic, chopped
  rough

¼ cup white wine
1 cup heavy whipping
  cream
½ cup whole pecans

Dust dolphin in flour seasoned with salt and white pepper; shake off excess. Add clarified butter to a skillet and heat to medium-high. Place dolphin and garlic in skillet and sauté until golden brown on both sides. Add wine to skillet and let reduce to half of original volume. Add cream and pecans, taste, and add salt and white pepper if desired. Transfer dolphin and sauce to a 1½-quart casserole dish and

bake in a preheated 350-degree oven for 15 to 20 minutes.
Serves 2.

SPEAKER'S CORNER'S ALMOND SPONGE CAKE

3 large eggs, room temperature
½ cup plus 1 tablespoon sugar
½ cup all-purpose flour
3 tablespoons butter, melted
1½ teaspoons almond
  extract

½ teaspoon vanilla
  extract
½ cup almonds,
  coarsely chopped
1 tablespoon
  confectioners' sugar

Separate eggs; beat yolks at high speed until they are a
light lemon color and have doubled in volume. Beat in ½
cup of sugar gradually. Mix in flour gradually. Add butter
and extracts and set aside. In separate bowl, beat egg whites
until foamy. Add a tablespoon of sugar and beat until stiff
peaks form. Carefully fold in egg-yolk mixture until completely incorporated. Gently fold in almonds by hand whip.
Pour into a 1-pound loaf pan and bake in a preheated 350-
degree oven for 25 to 30 minutes. Remove and let cool for 5
to 10 minutes. Run a knife around edge of pan and remove
cake. Sprinkle top with confectioners' sugar. Yields a 1-pound
sponge cake.

SPEAKER'S CORNER'S SHALLOT
BALSAMIC VINAIGRETTE

1 small shallot, chopped fine
1 clove garlic, minced
½ teaspoon Dijon mustard
1 teaspoon fresh basil,
  chopped fine
2 tablespoons champagne
  vinegar

2 tablespoons balsamic
  vinegar
3 ounces canola oil
3 ounces olive oil

Place shallot, garlic, mustard, basil, and vinegars into a
blender. Add the canola and olive oils and blend slowly. Toss
with assorted greens. Serves 4.

THE LAKESIDE INN
Mount Dora

THE LAKESIDE INN

Driving up to the Lakeside Inn on the shore of Lake Dora, thirty miles from Orlando, you breathe a sigh of contentment. Left behind are the city traffic and crowds, the tight schedules and frayed nerves. Here, in a town of quiet, hilly streets with lovely old homes and antique shops, at an inn with front-porch rocking chairs and enormous oaks draped with Spanish moss, the soul can restore itself.

The Lakeside Inn was built in 1883 as a ten-room hotel called the Alexander House. The country resort attracted Northern visitors eager for wintertime warmth and for the exotic wildlife and scenery found among Lake County's fourteen hundred lakes.

In the 1920s, the inn was in its heyday, offering popular music and entertainment and boating excursions. President Calvin Coolidge, who dedicated the hotel's two new wings in 1930, spent the winter at the inn after his term of office ended.

The Lakeside Inn underwent a $4-million award-winning restoration in the 1980s. The original wood floors and window casings were refurbished. Thirty-two coats of paint were removed from the exterior of the spacious frame hotel before it was painted "Flagler yellow." Though thoroughly modernized, with new tennis courts and a redone 1920s Olympic-size pool, the hotel has retained its original character.

A wide variety of fare is offered in the handsome Beauclaire Dining Room, with innovative specials daily. In addition to preparing such traditional favorites as Rack of Lamb and Châteaubriand, Chef Jon Koppenhofer has a flair for the unexpected. The Georgia Chicken is sautéed with a honey-bourbon glaze and roasted pecans; the Shrimp Madagascar is flavored with Pernod and green peppercorns and served on a bed of sautéed leeks and red peppers. Foods low in fat and cholesterol—such as Southwestern Trout, served with a homemade salsa—are marked with a heart.

As I enjoyed my dinner, I learned about the special events sponsored by the Lakeside Inn, such as the annual antique auto show and the Agatha Christie–style "Mystery Weekends." As appealing as those activities may be, the ambiance of the inn, so conducive to leisurely dining and good conversation, was enough to make me want to return.—B. R. M.

The Lakeside Inn is located at 100 South Alexander Street in Mount Dora. Breakfast is served from 7:00 until 10:30 a.m. daily. Lunch hours are 11:30 a.m. until 2:30 p.m. Monday through Friday and noon until 2:30 p.m. Saturday and Sunday. Dinner is served from 5:30 until 9:00 p.m. daily. For reservations (suggested), phone (904) 383-4101.

THE LAKESIDE INN'S ESCARGOTS

6 escargots
1 ounce shiitake mushroom, julienned
1 tablespoon butter
1 tablespoon shallots, minced
1 tablespoon parsley, chopped

salt and pepper
1 ounce Pinot Noir wine
2 ounces butter, softened
1 puff pastry shell, cooked

Rinse escargots well and hold. Sauté shiitake mushrooms in 1 tablespoon butter until tender; add shallots and cook until translucent. Add escargots, parsley, salt, and pepper. Deglaze with wine and slightly reduce. Add 2 ounces butter and swirl over low heat. Serve at once in precooked puff pastry shell. Serves 1.

THE LAKESIDE INN'S VEAL SORRENTO

2 thin slices prosciutto ham
2 3-ounce slices veal scaloppine
1 tablespoon butter
2 thin slices fontina cheese
1 ounce Marsala wine

2 ounces veal stock (canned beef broth may be substituted)
1 ounce butter, softened
Italian parsley for garnish

Gently pound prosciutto into one side of each veal cutlet.

83

Lightly dust the veal with flour, then sauté in 1 tablespoon butter until golden brown. Top with fontina cheese. Deglaze with wine and reduce. Add veal stock and reduce slightly. Add 1 ounce of butter and swirl on low heat. To serve, ladle the sauce over the veal and garnish with parsley. Serves 1.

THE LAKESIDE INN'S ATLANTIC SALMON

1 6-ounce salmon filet
1 tablespoon cracked
  black pepper
1 tablespoon butter
1 ounce cucumber, peeled,
  deseeded, and sliced
1 tablespoon shallots,
  minced

1 ounce white wine
3 ounces heavy cream
1 tablespoon sour cream
1 tablespoon chopped dill
salt and pepper

Encrust one side of salmon with peppercorns. Sear with butter in sauté pan, then place in a pie pan and bake at 350 degrees until flaky. Degrease the sauté pan and sauté cucumbers and shallots quickly. Deglaze with white wine and reduce 15 seconds on high. Add heavy cream and reduce to sauce consistency. Finish with sour cream, dill, salt, and pepper. Serves 1.

PARK PLAZA GARDENS
Winter Park

PARK PLAZA GARDENS

Winter Park is a unique town. Located in the heart of Florida, it's more Northeastern than tropical in architectural style. Sitting next door to Orlando, it seems far removed from the frantic hordes of Disney World. Winter Park's Main Street is real, with trees and small shops and businesses within walking distance.

And part of the charm of Winter Park is the Park Plaza Gardens restaurant. Rated consistently as one of the best restaurants in central Florida, Park Plaza Gardens is a culinary gem. Adjoining the beautifully restored European-style Park Plaza Hotel, the building now housing the restaurant was constructed in 1926. For years, it was a Winn-Lovett grocery store, then a Winn-Dixie. The original oak icebox can still be seen today, functioning as the refrigerator for the bar.

In what used to be a service entrance to the hotel, an enclosed brick courtyard has been built, complete with a glass ceiling. Here, diners sit amid ficus trees, ferns, and fresh flowers, enjoying good conversation and excellent cuisine in an elegant greenhouse setting.

In 1979, Park Plaza Gardens opened with an eighty-three-year-old chef who had cooked for five United States presidents. Ever since then, despite different ownerships, the restaurant has cultivated a tradition of hiring fine chefs and giving them room for creativity. Chef Stephen Gower is the latest talent to direct the cuisine.

Just reading the menu is a culinary inspiration, with appetizers like Crab Portobello—crabmeat sandwiched between portobello mushrooms, breaded and fried and served with a champagne leek buerre blanc—and Shrimp Tournedos Madras—shrimp wrapped in bacon and stuffed with mozzarella and wild mushrooms.

For entrées, absolutely fresh seafood is used in such dishes as Grouper Cabernaise. Two of my favorite meat dishes were Loin of Venison Syrah, sautéed with blackberries and finished with a syrah wine sauce, and Breast of Chicken Duvaly, stuffed with walnuts, apricots, dill, sour cream, and butter. For dessert, I passed up the Chocolate Profiteroles, but I couldn't resist ordering the Fresh Berries in a tulip-shaped pastry, topped with Lemon Sorbet. A beautiful finale.—B. R. M.

Park Plaza Gardens is located at 319 Park Avenue South in Winter Park. Lunch is served from 11:30 a.m. until 3:00 p.m. Monday through Saturday. Sunday brunch is served from 11:00 a.m. until 3:00 p.m. Dinner is served from 6:00 until 10:00 p.m. Sunday through Thursday and from 6:00 until 11:00 p.m. Friday and Saturday. For reservations (recommended), phone (407) 645-2475.

PARK PLAZA GARDENS'
RED SNAPPER BAKED WITH POTATO SCALES

1 6-ounce filet of snapper
1 large potato
1 cup beet juice
pinch of nutmeg
½ teaspoon cinnamon

pinch of arrowroot
(a thickener similar
to cornstarch)
1 stick hard butter
3 or 4 whole beets

Lightly flour snapper filet. Cut potato into a ¾-inch cylinder, then slice into thin slices; each slice should be about the size and thickness of a quarter. Lay the slices on the presentation side of the fish, overlapping to give an impression of scales. Lightly brown the fish potato side down in a nonstick pan with peanut oil. Turn over and brown the other side. Bake in a 400-degree oven for 4 to 5 minutes until fish is firm to the touch. To make the sauce, reduce the beet juice with nutmeg and cinnamon. Thicken with a small amount of arrowroot. Whisk in hard butter to finish. Serve the fish on top of the beet sauce and garnish with whole beets. Serves 1.

PARK PLAZA GARDENS' SHRIMP PROVENCALE

5 large shrimp
  (10-to-the-pound size),
  peeled and deveined
1 cup white wine
½ cup lemon juice
1 teaspoon shallots
1 teaspoon garlic
½ cup tomato concasse
  (peeled, seeded,
  and diced tomatoes)

1 teaspoon basil
1 teaspoon chopped
  parsley
½ cup butter
splash of Pernod

Sauté shrimp quickly in peanut oil. Drain oil; pour on wine and lemon juice. Add shallots, garlic, and tomato concasse. Simmer gently for 1 to 2 minutes. Add basil and parsley. Whisk in butter. Finish with a splash of Pernod. Adjust taste with salt and pepper if necessary. Serve over rice or pasta. Serves 1.

**LILI MARLENE'S AVIATORS
PUB AND RESTAURANT**
Orlando

LILI MARLENE'S AVIATORS PUB AND RESTAURANT

At Church Street Station in Orlando, the good times roll in a merry mix of food, drink, and entertainment modeled after days past.

Centered around the old train depot in downtown Orlando's historic district, Church Street Station fills more than a block on both sides of the street. The old depot, flanked by an antique steam engine on the tracks beside it, now houses antique and gift shops. A glorious Old West saloon, a hot-air balloon museum, and numerous bars and stores are anchored by Lili Marlene's Aviators Pub and Restaurant.

In the evening, the street is closed to traffic while antique cars, horse-drawn buggies, jugglers, and mimes create a carnival-like atmosphere. An admission fee charged after 5:00 p.m. admits you to the complex and to all the live shows, featuring country-and-western and Dixieland music as well as vaudeville and cancan acts.

Lili Marlene's Aviators Pub and Restaurant is a painstaking rejuvenation of the Strand Hotel, built in 1922. The restaurant glows with antique treasures collected by founder and entrepreneur Bob Snow during his world travels. The oak and beveled-glass doorway is from the famous Pace home in Pensacola. The heart-pine floors came from an old warehouse in New Orleans. The hand-carved oak booths where diners sit were church pews in a French Catholic church; the telephone booth was a confessional. The beautiful forty-foot bar and solid brass fans were recovered from a doomed Philadelphia hotel. The sixty-foot brass railing, made in 1903 and weighing five thousand pounds, came from the First National Bank of Atlanta.

In addition to this stunning array, authentic aviation memorabilia from World War I to the present day is suspended from the ceiling. Early radio broadcasts and the Lili Marlene World War II ballad are played in the background as diners bask in the nostalgia of it all.

The restaurant offers a wide range of lunch and dinner selections, specializing in Blackened Prime Rib and fresh Florida seafood. An extensive wine list is offered, as are flamboyant drinks like the Strawberry Daiquiri I indulged in.

For dinner, I enjoyed a scrumptious Scallop Mousseline and sampled the unusually good Baked Brie with Raspberry Vinaigrette. The special of the day, Veal Tips with Mushrooms and Burgundy Cream Sauce, was superb. After the delicious Chocolate Sponge Cake, I reluctantly had to race to the airport for my plane home. I would love to have lingered and viewed all the shows of Church Street Station.—B. R. M.

Lili Marlene's Aviators Pub and Restaurant is located in Church Street Station at 129 West Church Street in Orlando. Lunch is served daily from 11:00 a.m. until 4:00 p.m. and includes brunch items on Saturday and Sunday; dinner is served daily from 5:30 p.m. until midnight. For reservations (accepted), call (305) 422-2434.

LILI MARLENE'S
AVIATORS PUB AND RESTAURANT'S
BAKED BRIE WITH RASPBERRY VINAIGRETTE

3-ounce wedge Brie cheese
1 leaf puff pastry dough
1 egg yolk
1 tablespoon water
¼ ounce clarified butter
1 leaf of kale (optional)

1½ ounces Raspberry
   Vinaigrette Dressing
   (recipe below)
1 strawberry, hulled
2 slices kiwi fruit

Wrap Brie in puff pastry dough. Beat egg yolk with a little water for an egg wash. Dip pastry-wrapped Brie in egg wash. Brush baking pan with clarified butter; add Brie and bake at 350 degrees until done, about 5 to 7 minutes. If desired, place a leaf of kale on a plate. Ladle Raspberry Vinaigrette Dressing onto plate; place Brie on top. Garnish with whole strawberry and kiwi slices. Serves 1.

Raspberry Vinaigrette Dressing:
1 egg yolk
1½ cups vegetable oil
1⅙ cups raspberry vinegar

⅛ cup chopped
   shallots
salt and pepper to taste

91

Whip egg yolk until creamy. Add oil, then vinegar. Add shallots and seasonings and mix well. Store leftover dressing in the refrigerator; shake well before using. Yields 2½ cups.

LILI MARLENE'S
AVIATORS PUB AND RESTAURANT'S
CHICKEN, AVOCADO, AND BACON SALAD

2 to 3 lettuce leaves
4½ ounces cooked white
  chicken meat, diced
½ ounce crisply cooked
  bacon, chopped
½ ounce diced avocado

Tarragon Dressing
  (recipe follows)
2 avocado slices
seasonal fruit for garnish
1 tablespoon mango
  chutney

Line a plate with lettuce leaves. Mix chicken with some of the chopped bacon, the avocado, and Tarragon Dressing. Place this mixture in the center of the plate and top with the rest of the bacon and the avocado slices. Arrange fruit around the edges of the plate; accompany with mango chutney. Serves 1.

Tarragon Dressing:
2 ounces olive oil
1 ounce tarragon vinegar
1 teaspoon lemon juice
2 teaspoons Dijon
  mustard

1 tablespoon fresh
  tarragon
salt and pepper to taste

Whip all the ingredients together and pour over salad. Serves 1.

CHALET SUZANNE
Lake Wales

CHALET SUZANNE

Driving down Highway 17-A, in the middle of Florida citrus country, you'll suddenly see what appears to be a mirage. Reflected in a shimmering lake is the image of a pastel-colored European village. Even after you blink, the image will remain. If you're the curious type, you'll steer your car down a brick pathway toward the image. And you'll discover the Hinshaws' eclectically decorated country inn and restaurant, Chalet Suzanne.

In 1931, at the height of the Great Depression, the widowed Bertha Hinshaw ignored the skeptics who didn't believe that people would go out of their way for exceptional food and lodging. She established Chalet Suzanne, and for over fifty years repeat guests have proved that culinary ingenuity and charm will generally find an audience.

Chalet Suzanne is a mélange of not exactly offbeat, but off-measured, buildings. After a fire, the Hinshaws' horse stable, rabbit hutch, and chicken houses were patched together to form the meandering village. Whether they're painted pink or blue or lavender, you'll find the varied spiral- and rectangular-shaped buildings studded with ornamental ceramic tiles that define a corner, a window, or a courtyard entrance. Bertha Hinshaw even preferred the beautiful tiles to tablecloths, so many of the dining-room tables feature unusual tile patterns. Not only is each tabletop different, so are the sets of crystal, the fine china, the candlesticks, and the fresh floral arrangements.

Bertha's son Carl, a World War II pilot, inherited his late mother's culinary ability. His special soups have even been sent with the Apollo 15 and 16 crews to the moon. The family's cannery will ship some soups home for you, too, if you like.

Sitting with a view of the lake, I began my meal with Carl's creation of Cream of Romaine Soup and immediately understood why it is a NASA favorite. After consuming too many little Potato Rolls, I deglazed my palate with a Lemon and Champagne Sorbet. For my entrée, I was considering Shrimp Curry or Lobster Newburg until Carl's wife, Vita, advised

94

that while Carl never gives out his recipe for Chicken Suzanne, I should try it anyway. I did, and was only sorry that I hadn't arrived hungrier, as they serve deliciously large portions.

I was going to refuse dessert, but the friendly Scandinavian-costumed waitresses coaxed me into trying Gâteau Christina—a definite died-and-gone-to-heaven dessert.

At bedtime, my sherbet-colored bedroom suite added to the delight of finding such luxury tucked within the citrus belt. And the next morning, breakfast began with Vita Hinshaw's invention of Broiled Grapefruit with cinnamon and sugar—perfect anywhere!

Chalet Suzanne is located off U.S. 27 on Highway 17-A in Lake Wales. Meals are served from 8:00 a.m. until 9:30 p.m. daily. The restaurant is closed on Mondays from May through December. For reservations (suggested), call (813) 676-6011.

CHALET SUZANNE'S VEAL CHOPS

1½ sticks or more butter
2 medium-size onions, sliced
2 cups sliced fresh mushrooms
½ teaspoon celery salt
½ cup dry vermouth
salt and pepper to taste
flour for dusting

4 6- to 8-ounce veal chops
2 cups chicken broth (homemade or commercial)
1 cup or more sour cream
½ pound pasta, cooked
2 or more bananas, sliced
brown sugar to taste

Melt 2 to 3 tablespoons of the butter in a skillet and sauté onions until tender; set aside. Add 3 to 4 tablespoons of butter to the skillet and sauté mushrooms until barely tender; sprinkle them with celery salt and set aside with onions. Deglaze the skillet with a little vermouth, then pour the remaining vermouth over onions and mushrooms. Salt, pepper, and lightly dust the veal on both sides. Melt 4 tablespoons butter in the skillet and brown veal on both sides. Add chicken broth to the veal; cover and bake in a 300-degree oven for about 40 minutes. Add mushrooms, onions, and sour cream and bake until heated through. Serve over seasoned pasta.

In a separate skillet, melt 2 or more tablespoons butter and quickly sauté the banana slices, sprinkled with brown sugar, until brown. Arrange on plates with veal and pasta. Serves 4.

CHALET SUZANNE'S GATEAU CHRISTINA

Meringue:

4 egg whites	⅓ cup blanched
1½ cups sugar	ground almonds

Preheat oven to 250 degrees. Cut aluminum foil into 4 8-inch circles and grease each lightly. Whip egg whites until stiff, gradually adding sugar and almonds as eggs begin to stiffen. Place foil rounds on a large baking sheet and spread each evenly with meringue. Bake for 15 minutes or until meringue is dry. Carefully turn meringues over and bake 5 minutes longer.

Chocolate filling:

2 egg whites	2 sticks butter,
½ cup sugar	softened
2 tablespoons	4 ounces semisweet
sweetened cocoa	chocolate, melted

In the top of a double boiler, over hot (not boiling) water, beat egg whites until foamy. Gradually add sugar, cocoa, butter, and chocolate, beating until thick and creamy. Remove from heat and cool.

To assemble gâteau, place the best meringue layer on the bottom and spread with chocolate. Top with another meringue, pressing down lightly to make layers fit together. Spread with chocolate. Repeat until all meringues are used and the top is liberally coated with chocolate. Cover and refrigerate for at least 24 hours. Yields 1 4-layered gâteau.

Note: These may be stored in tin boxes for gifts.

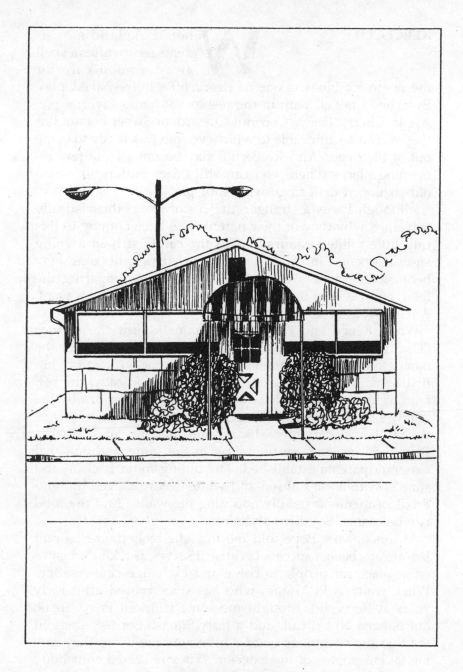

REECECLIFF
Lakeland

REECECLIFF

When Lakeland's residents return after a spell away, a good cure for the homesick blues is one of Reececliff's home-baked pies. Everyone I talked with in the restaurant had a favorite pie: Apple, Cherry, Peach, Coconut Custard, or Sweet Potato. But they were also agreeable to whichever pie was ready to come out of the oven. And Reececliff may be one of the few remaining places where you can still order buttermilk or an old-fashioned malt to go with your pie.

Although I was a stranger, the customers enthusiastically explained why they or their parents had been coming to this tidy little white restaurant with the candy-striped awning since it opened in 1934. I was told that people come here because the owners don't take shortcuts in preparing the food, and because they listen to what their customers want. A recipe for success in any city.

When Reece and Clifford Stidham bought the former "Ducky Wucky" drive-in restaurant, they didn't care for the name, so the couple combined his first name with half of her first name to form the name *Reececliff*. Periodically, the restaurant has been remodeled, and it is now being run by the family's third generation, Robert Pope. Robert insists, just as the Stidhams' daughter Mildred and her husband, Charlie Pope, had insisted, on operating in the same tradition that his grandparents established. The dining room is clean and simple, with a kind of red-and-white décor relieved by hundreds of menus tastefully adorning the walls. And the food is wholesome, Southern-style fare.

At lunch, Mrs. Pope told me that she feels the restaurant has always been a success because it serves as a kind of gathering place for people to come and exchange conversation. When waitress Jo Young, who has since retired after forty years at Reececliff, brought me some Chicken Fried Steak, hot Banana Nut Bread, and a tasty Squash Soufflé, she told me that the customers were a little nervous when they saw me taking photos of the exterior. "They're scared somebody new will come in here and change everything. It wouldn't be the same without this family." I believed her.

It would have been a sacrilege to leave without tasting one of their pies. After great deliberation, I finally chose the Cherry Pie. It was perfect, not too tart or sweet.

My lunch may sound unpretentious, just as Reececliff is, but when you taste the food, you'll know why the restaurant has lasted. While I was there, I saw a customer bring a beautiful bouquet of pink camellias to the restaurant. The incident reminded me a little of taking flowers to a friend. In fact, that's just what it was.

Reececliff is located at 940 South Florida Avenue in Lakeland. Meals are served from 9:00 a.m. until 10:00 p.m. Monday through Saturday. Reservations are unnecessary, but the telephone number is (813) 686-6661.

REECECLIFF'S SQUASH SOUFFLE

2 pounds fresh yellow
  squash, chopped
1 small onion, chopped
15⅓ ounces evaporated
  milk
1 teaspoon salt
2 tablespoons melted
  butter (no substitutes)

2 eggs, beaten
2 tablespoons sugar
pepper to taste
¼ pound cheddar
  cheese, grated
¾ cup ground potato
  chips or crackers

Steam squash and onions together until tender. Place in a bowl and add milk, salt, butter, eggs, sugar, pepper, and cheese. Mix until well blended and place in a greased 8-by-10-inch pan. Top with potato chips or crackers. Bake in a preheated 325-degree oven for 45 minutes. Serves 12.

REECECLIFF'S CHERRY PIE

1 9-inch piecrust
½ cup cherry juice
1 cup sugar
¼ teaspoon salt

1 tablespoon cornstarch
1 tablespoon all-purpose
   flour
2 cups cherries, drained

Prepare a piecrust using your favorite recipe. Make a little extra dough to use as strips across the top of the pie. In a bowl, combine cherry juice, sugar, salt, cornstarch, and flour and stir until smooth. Fold in cherries and pour this mixture into the piecrust. Take strips of dough and lace across the top in lattice fashion, securing the ends by pressing them into the piecrust. Bake in a preheated 325-degree oven for 45 minutes. Yields 1 pie.

REECECLIFF'S BANANA NUT BREAD

½ cup vegetable oil
1 cup sugar
2 eggs
2 cups all-purpose flour

1 teaspoon soda
½ teaspoon salt
2 large bananas, crushed
½ cup pecans (optional)

Cream oil, sugar, and eggs together until smooth. Add flour gradually with soda and salt. Fold in bananas and mix until well combined. Mix in pecans if desired. Pour into a greased and floured 1-pound loaf pan and bake in a 325-degree oven for 45 minutes. Check to see if bread is done; if not, bake an additional 5 minutes or so. Yields 1 loaf.

THE COLUMBIA
Tampa

THE COLUMBIA

The Columbia, in Tampa's historic Ybor City, combines robust Spanish food, dramatic architecture, traditional Latin entertainment, and Old World courtliness to create a cultural adventure not to be missed. Proudly proclaimed the oldest restaurant in Florida and the oldest and largest Spanish restaurant in the United States, the Columbia has been in the same family for four generations.

The present-day Columbia covers an entire city block. It has eleven rooms, with a seating capacity of 1,660. It also has its own commissary, coffee mill, and laundry.

It all began in 1905, when Casimiro Hernandez, Sr., a Cuban immigrant, opened a coffee shop and bar. Tampa's cigar industry was in its heyday in Ybor City then, and the thousands of Spanish-speaking residents outnumbered the English-speaking population. The cafe soon became a favorite of locals, and a new dining room had to be added in 1920.

After the death of the elder Hernandez in 1929, his son Casimiro Hernandez, Jr., took over the management. In 1935, under his direction, the Columbia became the first restaurant in Florida to be air-conditioned. In 1936, Hernandez built the richly ornate Don Quixote Dining Room, with its splendid crystal chandelier. The next year, he added more rooms and a two-story glass-roofed interior courtyard, complete with a balcony and a sculptured fountain, still a focal point of the restaurant today.

A great admirer of the famous Spanish writer Cervantes, Hernandez commissioned Tampa artist Sergio de Meza to paint scenes from *Don Quixote*. Every day for thirty years, the artist ate three meals a day at the Columbia, producing seventy-nine paintings of Don Quixote as well as impressive copies of old masters. Many of these paintings hang on the walls of the vast restaurant today.

Cesar Gonzmart, married to Hernandez's only child, Adela, entered the family business in 1953 and expanded the restaurant even more. Branches were opened in Sarasota in 1959 and St. Augustine in 1983; they are run by sons Casey and Richard.

102

Until his death in 1992, Gonzmart personally greeted guests throughout his restaurant. Many customers recall Gonzmart—an accomplished musician who once served as concertmaster of the Havana Symphony—thrilling audiences with occasional violin performances. His family carries on the rich traditions of the Columbia.

Numerous customers have come weekly, even daily, for years to enjoy traditional Spanish favorites like Cuban Black Bean Soup, Chilled Gazpacho, Chicken and Yellow Rice "Ybor," Cuban-Style Steak, and Snapper Alicante.

More than fifteen hundred articles have been written about the Columbia in its nearly ninety years of existence. For many, it is the symbol of the city of Tampa. The night I visited, a French television station was filming the flamenco dancers for a documentary on Tampa. The castanets, pounding feet, and swirling skirts, the delicious sangria, and the warmth and drama of the décor made for a perfect television clip, and for a perfect evening.—B. R. M.

The Columbia is located at 2117 East Seventh Avenue in Tampa's Ybor City historic district. It is open daily for lunch and dinner from 11:00 a.m. until 11:00 p.m. On Sunday, a Cuban feast begins at noon. For reservations, call (813) 248-4961.

THE COLUMBIA'S SNAPPER ALICANTE

2 ½-pound snapper filets	pinch of white pepper
1 onion, cut in round slices	½ cup brown gravy
2 green peppers, cut in rings	½ cup white wine
12 almonds	Shrimp Supreme
¼ cup olive oil	(recipe below)
½ teaspoon salt	4 slices breaded eggplant

Note: Before you begin preparing the snapper, marinate the shrimp for the Shrimp Supreme (see instructions below).

In a casserole (preferably clay), place snapper filets on top of the onion slices. Top with pepper rings and almonds. Pour the olive oil, salt, pepper, brown gravy, and white wine over fish. Bake uncovered at 350 degree for 25 minutes. Meanwhile, prepare the Shrimp Supreme and fry the eggplant. Garnish baked snapper with shrimp and eggplant. Serves 2.

Shrimp Supreme:

4 large shrimp, shelled   **1 egg**
¼ cup lemon juice   **¼ cup milk**
salt and pepper to taste   **½ cup flour**
2 strips bacon, cut in half   **fat or oil for frying**

Marinate the shrimp in lemon juice, salt, and pepper for 1 hour. Wrap marinated shrimp with a half-slice of bacon each; skewer bacon in place with a toothpick. Mix egg and milk into a batter. Dip shrimp in batter, then roll in flour. Deep-fry in fat until golden brown.

THE COLUMBIA'S
CHICKEN AND YELLOW RICE "YBOR"

1 3-pound chicken   **2 cups long-grain rice**
½ cup olive oil   **1 bay leaf**
2 onions, chopped   **1 tablespoon salt**
1 green pepper, chopped   **(or less if desired)**
2 medium-size tomatoes,   **¼ cup white wine**
  peeled, seeded, and chopped **½ cup small green peas**
2 cloves garlic, minced   **(frozen or canned)**
4 cups chicken broth   **2 pimientos, cut in half**
½ teaspoon saffron   **4 asparagus tips**

Cut the fryer into quarters. In a skillet, sauté chicken in heated olive oil until the skin is golden. Remove chicken and place in a casserole. In the same oil, sauté onions, green peppers, tomatoes, and garlic for 5 minutes. Pour over chicken. Add chicken broth, saffron, rice, bay leaf, and salt to the skillet. When it begins to boil, pour mixture over the other ingredients in the casserole. Cover casserole and bake in a 350-degree oven for 20 minutes. Take the dish out of the oven, sprinkle it with wine, and garnish with peas, pimientos, and asparagus tips. Serves 4.

VALENCIA GARDEN
Tampa

VALENCIA GARDEN "Salud and happy days," said Manuel Beiro every night for fifteen years as he advertised his Spanish restaurant on live television. The Valencia Garden ad, which may hold the record for the world's longest continuously running live-television commercial, is still remembered by Tampa residents who have long forgotten the "Shock Theater" shows it sponsored.

Manuel Beiro opened his Valencia Garden restaurant in Tampa in 1927. Born in Spain near Santiago de Compostela, he decorated his restaurant with murals of his beloved homeland, painted by noted artist Harry Bierce. The mayor of Seville personally sent him the tiles used below the artwork. The restaurant's equally authentic Spanish food attracted a faithful following in Tampa's Hispanic community.

David Agliano, the founder's grandson, now manages a greatly expanded Valencia Garden. He recalls with fondness his grandparents, who lived upstairs in the house behind the restaurant. "My grandmother Rose did everything around here," he said. "She called the restaurant her 'little house' and would put out flowers and sweep the parking lot. The two of them worked seven days a week, every day of the year. My grandmother was always one to make you laugh. The restaurant was like a warm and inviting home."

Though the restaurant now seats three hundred in numerous rooms, David Agliano still tries to preserve that personal touch. He has no maître d' at lunch, but seats everyone himself, talking with regulars who have come to Valencia Garden for years for traditional "Tampa Spanish" food.

The menu includes such favorites as Arroz con Pollo, Paella, Cuban Black Bean Soup, Ropa Vieja (shredded beef with onions and tomatoes), and Papillot (fish stuffed with shrimp and lobster and baked in French paper). I began my lunch with Caldo Gallego, a hearty soup made with ham hocks and turnip greens—a treat for a Southern girl like me. The Shrimp Ajillo that followed was delicious, as was the Cuban Bread.

My waiter, employed at Valencia Garden since 1953—he served the food on that television ad!—was eager for me to try their Crema Española. David Agliano told me that his restaurant is one of the very few to offer this difficult-to-perfect dessert. So I took "just one more bite" and was glad I did. It was superb.—B. R. M.

Valencia Garden is located at 811 West John F. Kennedy Boulevard in Tampa. Lunch is served from 11:00 a.m. until 2:30 p.m. Monday through Friday; dinner is served from 5:00 until 10:00 p.m. Monday through Saturday. For reservations (not required), call (813) 253-3773.

VALENCIA GARDEN'S CREMA ESPANOLA

1 cup light cream	3 cups milk
¼ cup flour	8 egg yolks
1 cup sugar	1 tablespoon butter
1½ teaspoons vanilla	

Topping:
½ cup sugar   1 teaspoon cinnamon

Mix cream, flour, sugar, and vanilla in a mixing bowl with a hand beater. Meanwhile, bring milk to a boil. Add hot milk to cream mixture and beat with a hand mixer until smooth. Cook the mixture in the top pot of a double boiler until thickened. In a mixing bowl, beat egg yolks until smooth. Pour hot mixture into eggs, stirring rapidly. Return mixture to double boiler and add butter. Cook 25 to 35 minutes, stirring frequently. Pour mixture into a 1½-quart glass serving dish. Cool.

Combine ½ cup sugar and cinnamon. Sprinkle mixture on top of cooled cream. (For burnt or caramelized topping at home, you can place the dish under the broiler until topping is brown.) Refrigerate. Serves 6.

VALENCIA GARDEN'S CALDO GALLEGO

1 1½-pound ham hock
½ pound lean beef
½ pound salt pork
1 bunch turnip greens
dash of nutmeg
1 cup Great Northern
  white beans, soaked
  and drained
1 onion, chopped
1 green pepper,
  chopped

1 clove garlic,
  minced
3 tablespoons bacon
  grease
3 potatoes, peeled
  and cubed
2 chorizos
salt to taste

In a 4-quart pot, place ham hock, beef, and pork. Cover with water and bring to a boil. Skim several times. Cook over medium heat until tender, about 1 hour. Chop greens and add to meat. Add nutmeg and beans. Cook uncovered on low heat for 30 minutes. In a skillet, sauté onions, green peppers, and garlic in bacon grease. Add to soup. Add potatoes, chorizos, and salt. Cover and cook 45 minutes longer, until potatoes are done. Serves 6.

THE MARITANA IN THE DON CESAR
St. Petersburg Beach

THE MARITANA IN
THE DON CESAR

The pink spires and barrel tile roof of the majestic Don CeSar Beach Resort can be seen for miles, a rosy-hued beacon by land or by sea. Looking at the imposing beauty of this tribute to romanticism and perseverance, it's hard to imagine that twenty-five years ago there were people who wanted to destroy it, to tear it down for a public park.

This lack of vision wouldn't have surprised the man who built the Don CeSar in the first place, back around 1925. Against the advice of everyone, Thomas J. Rowe, who moved from Virginia to Florida for health reasons, purchased a desolate eighty-acre tract of land on the inaccessible island of Pass-a-Grille, near St. Petersburg.

Inspired by the architecture of George Merrick's Coral Gables, James Deering's Vizcaya, and Addison Mizner's Palm Beach and Boca Raton, Rowe turned the wilderness into a subdivision of Mediterranean-style homes. For the crowning glory of his development, he lavished $1,250,000 on a magnificent hotel. He named it the Don CeSar, after Don Caesar, the leading character in his favorite American opera, *Maritana*.

The hotel was built on shifting beach sand by using a floating pad of concrete and pyramided footings so thick and strong that they have yet to show any signs of settling.

After a glorious gala opening on January 16, 1928, and a few prosperous years, during which the hotel was open only for "the season" of January and February, the Great Depression took its toll. Famous patrons such as F. Scott Fitzgerald and his wife, Zelda, novelist Faith Baldwin, attorney Clarence Darrow, and the entire New York Yankees baseball team came and went.

The army took over the hotel in 1942 as a hospital. It became the Air Force Convalescent Center in 1944, then the Veterans Administration Regional Office. With each change, more and more of the once-luxurious interior was stripped and institutionalized. The overall appearance deteriorated, and in 1969 the building was abandoned, left to vandals and pigeons.

Amid cries of "Tear the eyesore down!" writer June Hurley

Young started to publicize the building's plight. In 1971, hotelier William Bowman, Jr., accepted the challenge of restoring the Don CeSar, a job that required twelve thousand gallons of flamingo pink paint and the removal and replacement, pane by pane, of thirteen thousand pieces of glass to refinish the windows.

The second gala opening of the Don CeSar was held on November 24, 1973, to the delight of the community. Since then, millions more have been spent over the years to modernize the interior and add the latest amenities.

The Maritana Grille, located on the first floor of the hotel, is a dining adventure. The blue room is surrounded by saltwater tropical-fish aquariums and hand-painted murals of moonlit beach scenes. The menu is "Floribbean" cuisine, with many specialties prepared over a pecan- and cherry-wood grill. Chef Bryan Dillon's Fire-Roasted Gulf Fish with Flaming Herbs is an especially dramatic entrée.—B. R. M.

The Maritana Grille is located in the Don CeSar Beach Resort at 3400 Gulf Boulevard in St. Petersburg Beach. Dinner is served from 5:30 until 10:00 p.m. Monday through Thursday and from 5:30 until 11:00 p.m. Friday and Saturday. For reservations (suggested), phone (813) 360-1881.

THE MARITANA'S SEARED YELLOWFIN TUNA

8 ounces yellowfin tuna
1 teaspoon ground
  black pepper
½ cup chopped cilantro
2 tablespoons chopped
  shallots
1 cup olive oil

½ teaspoon chopped
  garlic
½ teaspoon paprika
pinch of blackening
  spice

Cut tuna into strips 1 inch square. Keep fish cold. Mix all dry ingredients with oil. Let sit for half an hour. Take tuna from refrigerator and add to mixture. Pack pepper and herb mixture around tuna. Sear in a cast-iron skillet on top of stove, very fast and very hot, to rare. Let cool. To serve, slice tuna very thin and place around the rim of a plate. Garnish with Jicama Salad and Wasabi Dressing (recipes below).

THE MARITANA'S JICAMA SALAD

2 large jicama, julienned
1 red pepper, julienned
¼ of a red onion, julienned
segments of 2 oranges
6 tablespoons chopped cilantro
6 tablespoons chopped parsley

salt and pepper to taste
pinch of sugar
½ teaspoon sesame oil
1 tablespoon olive oil
juice from 3 oranges
juice from 2 lemons

In a large bowl, combine the cut vegetables, orange segments, cilantro, and parsley. Season with salt, pepper, and sugar. Add oils and juices. Must be served chilled.

THE MARITANA'S WASABI DRESSING

2 ounces wasabi paste
   (a very hot Japanese
   horseradish)
¾ cup rice wine vinegar
2 tablespoons minced
   parsley
pinch of sugar

2 tablespoons minced
   cilantro
½ teaspoon Dijon
   mustard
3 cups olive oil
½ teaspoon sesame
   oil

Combine wasabi, vinegar, and all dry ingredients in a bowl. Blend in mustard. Slowly add oils until blended. Serve chilled. Serves 8 to 10.

COLEY'S
Sarasota

COLEY'S

When George Prime built his hardware store in downtown Sarasota in 1915, I'm sure he never dreamed that it would one day be Sarasota's hangout for the theater crowd. But after Prohibition, the hardware store was converted into a bar called the Circus Bar. In other regions of the country, the word *circus* might have various connotations, but in Sarasota, the winter quarters of the Ringling Brothers Circus, it had only one.

John Ringling and his wife, Mable, moved here in 1890 and built their famed winter estate, a combination of architectural styles ranging from Neo-Gothic Venetian to Italian Renaissance. Ringling also built a hotel called the Ringling Towers for his circus stars. The hotel is gone, but Ringling's stunning estate, now an immense art museum, is worth a visit. It houses what is considered one of the finest Baroque art collections in America. You can also see Ringling's *Ca 'd' Zan*—"House of John"—with its frescoed ceilings, marble baths, and other remarkable signatures of that opulent age. People of all ages, whether circus buffs or not, will also enjoy the circus museum, erected in 1948 to hold circus art and memorabilia.

I suspect that many of Ringling's performers frequented the Circus Bar, just as these days local theater actors and audiences hang out at Coley's before and after shows. The restaurant has several sections, each with a different personality. In the front room, skylights and lots of flowing greenery make a bright and airy place for lunch, or you may prefer a seat at the bar, where you can view all the liquor stored in the old oak dairy bar. The mounted deer head above the bar will no doubt be wearing the hat of the season, or perhaps one from a current theatrical production. The bar and the back room both have a pressed-tin ceiling brought from a bar in Rochester, New York. The back room, with its exposed brick walls, is decorated with old portraits in heavy gilt frames and with hanging Tiffany lamps.

I sat at a booth in the back room and people-watched as I sampled their crunchy Beer Batter Fried Zucchini, an imported beer, and a fresh salad mixed with their multipurpose Dill Dressing. I tried a bit of the dressing on Chicken Wings, Potato Skins, and even Char-Broiled Shrimp. The taste varies but works with each one. Then it was time for some of their "not too spicy" Chili, which was made with lots of meat and served with some terrific French garlic bread. For me, lunch is a bit too early for Spanish Coffee, but next time—say, after a play—I'll try that intriguing concoction.

Coley's is located at 1355 Main Street in Sarasota. Meals are served from 11:30 a.m. until 2:00 a.m. Monday through Saturday. Sunday meals are served from 5:00 p.m. until 2:00 a.m. For reservations (suggested), call (813) 955-5627.

COLEY'S CHILI

2 to 3 tablespoons butter	pinch of cayenne pepper
1 pound ground chuck	1 16-ounce can whole
2 green peppers, seeded	tomatoes in juice
and diced	1 16-ounce can crushed
1 large Spanish onion, diced	tomatoes
¼ teaspoon garlic salt	1 16-ounce can red
½ teaspoon chili powder	kidney beans

In a large Dutch oven, melt butter and brown meat with peppers and onions until vegetables are tender. Drain grease from pan. Add garlic salt, chili powder, and cayenne pepper, stirring until well mixed. Add cans of tomatoes and kidney beans and stir until mixed. Lower heat to medium-low and cook for about an hour and a half, stirring frequently. Adjust seasonings if desired. Serves 8.

COLEY'S BEER BATTER FRIED ZUCCHINI

2 large zucchini
2 cups self-rising flour
5 tablespoons butter, melted
2 eggs
8 ounces regular domestic beer

pinch of salt
pinch of white pepper
pinch of garlic salt
4 drops of lemon juice
oil for deep-frying

Wash zucchini and slice ¼-inch thick on the diagonal; cover and set aside. With an electric mixer, mix flour with butter and eggs. Add beer, mixing until combined. Add spices and lemon juice and mix for about 10 minutes. Heat oil in a deep fryer until hot. Hand-dip zucchini in batter and deep-fry in oil for about 3 to 5 minutes until golden brown. Serves 4.

CABBAGE KEY INN AND RESTAURANT
Bokeelia

CABBAGE KEY INN AND RESTAURANT

The thing to do on Cabbage Key is nothing, but you'll learn to do it well. You'll even flirt with the idea of chucking civilization altogether. Since you can only get here by boat, and since there are no telephones or television sets, you relearn socializing. Here, the people you meet are the amenities.

It was, no doubt, the isolation that convinced famed mystery writer Mary Roberts Rinehart and her family to build a home here in the 1930s, high above an Indian shell mound. Decades ahead of her time, Rinehart put a solar heating system on the roof of this enduring Bermuda-style home.

In the thirties, you might have run into Rinehart's fishing buddy, Ernest Hemingway. The best tarpon in the Intracoastal Waterway lured him and the often-reclusive Rinehart to fish here daily. If you aren't a "do nothinger" like me, it's still the place for tarpon and sailing.

The view from my pine-paneled bedroom showed the purple-blue iridescent waters where, during the boat trip, I had watched dolphins frolic as endangered species of birds soared and dipped overhead. After dropping my luggage, I settled in at the bar and was introduced to a Cabbage Creeper. One of these drinks will take the edge off a travel-weary soul, but too many Creepers could whittle you down to something with the mental capacity of the plant in the drink's name.

It was near sunset, so owner Rob Wells took me for an island tour, explaining that most of the dense primeval vegetation has been here since the Calusa Indians inhabited the islands. Archaeological finds from the shell mounds date man's existence here from about 145 B.C. The once-dominant Calusa tribe, known for its highly developed art, also engaged in ritualistic human sacrifice around 1200 A.D., normally with captives taken in battle. But attack from the Spanish and northern Indians dissolved the tribe, except for a few who found their way to the Everglades and Cuba.

You can change for dinner if you like, but your comfort is what matters. In the back dining room, which gives the feel of being in the jungle, I sat at a long table beside one of the last Calusas, dockmaster Terry Forgie. My appetizer of Char-

Broiled Shrimp, prepared with Sanibel Pinks, was without equal, which is probably why I ate it so fast.

I had a terrific Sautéed Grouper, then other guests shared the Stone Crab Claws with me. This dish just may be the restaurant's best. But any shrimp devotee is going to be pleased with the Spatatini Noodles with Sanibel Pinks. The dish has a fresh, lemony trace to enhance it. And you must never go to Cabbage Key without having the frozen Key Lime Pie. Freezing is the catalyst for its superb taste.

The next morning, winding down the conch shell–lined walk to the dock, I realized that when you spend time here, you are revitalized by doing nothing but absorbing the peace and tropical beauty of this very special place. One night here isn't enough; you'll want more.

Cabbage Key Inn and Restaurant is located off Bokeelia. Breakfast is served from 7:30 until 9:00 a.m. Monday through Saturday and until 10:00 a.m. on Sunday. Lunch is served from 11:30 a.m. until 3:00 p.m. Monday through Friday and until 4:00 p.m. on Saturday and 6:00 p.m. on Sunday. Dinner is served from 6:00 until 8:30 p.m. Monday through Saturday and until 7:00 p.m. Sunday. To arrange transportation and reservations, call (813) 283-2278.

CABBAGE KEY'S CHAR-BROILED SHRIMP

3 sticks margarine
3 sticks butter
¼ cup sherry
¼ cup lemon juice
4 ounces fresh garlic,
   puréed

pinch of thyme
pinch of oregano
3 pounds shrimp, peeled
   and deveined

Melt margarine and butter on low heat. Add sherry, lemon juice, garlic, thyme, and oregano. Remove pan from heat and let cool to room temperature. Add shrimp to the pan and let marinate about 1 hour. Sauté shrimp until half-done (about a minute). Finish shrimp over the open flame of an outside barbecue grill. Serve with melted butter. Serves 8 to 10.

119

CABBAGE KEY'S CHICKEN

4 boneless chicken breasts
salt to taste
white pepper to taste
flour for dusting
3 tablespoons
   Key Lime Butter
   (recipe below), divided

18 to 20 mushrooms,
   sliced
4 sprigs parsley,
4 ounces white wine
½ pound cooked rice
   or noodles

Flatten chicken to an even thickness by tapping with a mallet. Lightly salt and pepper both sides. Dust lightly with flour. Heat 1½ tablespoons Key Lime Butter in a skillet and sauté chicken on both sides. Place chicken on warm plates. Add remaining butter to the skillet and sauté mushrooms with parsley. Stir in white wine and let the sauce reduce on low heat until it begins to thicken. Pour sauce over chicken and serve with rice or noodles. Serves 4.

Key Lime Butter:
2 sticks butter
1 ounce Key lime juice

¼ bunch parsley,
   minced

Soften butter and mix with lime juice and parsley until well blended. Yields 1 cup.

CABBAGE KEY'S HOUSE DRESSING

1 teaspoon Dijon mustard
1 teaspoon horseradish
¾ cup red wine vinegar
¼ cup vegetable oil

salt and pepper to taste
2 tablespoons blue
   cheese, crumbled

Whisk together mustard and horseradish. Gradually add vinegar, and without stopping, slowly add oil. Whisk vigorously until smooth. Add salt and pepper to taste, then whisk in the cheese. Yields 1 cup.

KING'S CROWN DINING ROOM
Captiva Island

KING'S CROWN DINING ROOM

Long before Ponce de Leon dropped anchor in San Carlos Bay in 1513, Captiva was the site of Native American settlements. Though Captiva and Sanibel together were known as Costa de Carocoles—"Coast of the Seashells"—Captiva derives its name from the nefarious doings of the pirate Jose Gaspar. The pirate and his band caused a reign of terror in the 1880s by kidnapping people, mostly women, and holding the captives for ransom on the island.

The island also attracted its share of homesteaders in the 1880s. At the tip of the island, where South Seas Plantation is now, Tobe Bryant grew sugarcane, avocados, and Key limes. The produce was kept in a warehouse that has now been magnificently renovated for the King's Crown Dining Room. The old warehouse was ideally located just a few yards from the docks. It was here that workers loaded the fruits and vegetables that were shipped to New York and other ports.

The entrance to the King's Crown Dining Room is almost obscured by dense vegetation. Except for the old fireplace, the inside gives not a hint that it once functioned as a warehouse. Now, stained-glass windows, crystal chandeliers, and mauve print draperies are as inviting as the ocean views.

The lovely pink linen tablecloths and delicate floral china could enhance any dish. My companion and I began with an appetizer of Shrimp with Stone-Ground Mustard Cream. Those big Sanibel pink shrimp are like no other shrimp, and the tart mustard sauce gave them a flavor that definitely opened the taste buds.

We then moved on to Salmon en Croute. Salmon, considered a brain food, is also a marvel for the palate. With its vegetable mélange, dominated by wild mushrooms and a rich Cabernet Sauce, this is about as succulent as a dish can get. The Strawberry and Kiwi Flambé is prepared tableside. This is entertaining to watch, and like food cooked over a campfire, it somehow just seems to taste better.

I found the King's Crown, in its lush tropical setting, to be like a glittering jewel—reflecting gastronomical as well as visual rays.

King's Crown Dining Room is located in South Seas Plantation at the end of Captiva Road on Captiva Island. Dinner is served from 5:30 until 9:30 p.m. daily from Christmas to June and Tuesday through Saturday from June to Christmas. For reservations (suggested), call (813) 472-5111, ext. 3359.

KING'S CROWN DINING ROOM'S SALMON EN CROUTE

Vegetable Stuffing:

2 to 3 tablespoons butter
½ medium onion, julienned
½ red pepper, julienned
1 ear of corn, kernels cut
   from cob

2 cups wild mushrooms
   (may use shiitake, oyster,
   lobster, or chanterelle)
salt and pepper
   to taste

Melt butter in a sauté pan over medium-high heat and sauté vegetables only until crunchy. Season with salt and pepper. Set aside to cool.

Cabernet Sauce:

8 ounces red wine
½ teaspoon black pepper
1¼ teaspoons fresh
   rosemary, minced

8 ounces cold butter,
   cubed
salt and pepper
   to taste

Place wine, pepper, and rosemary in a saucepan over medium-high heat and reduce to ¼ original volume. Remove from heat and gradually whisk in butter a cube at a time. Add salt and pepper. Set aside and keep warm.

Salmon:

20 sheets or more
   phyllo pastry
8 ounces butter, melted
4 6-ounce salmon filets,
   sliced thin
2 cups Vegetable
   Stuffing (recipe above)

8 ounces Cabernet
   Sauce (recipe above)
1 egg
2 tablespoons water

Place 1 piece of phyllo down on clean work surface and brush with butter. Place another sheet over it and brush each alternating sheet with butter, continuing until there are 5 sheets. Place 1 filet onto pastry large enough to fold over. Top with ½ cup Vegetable Stuffing, or enough to cover filet. Ladle Cabernet Sauce over top of stuffing. Fold the sheet together, sealing like an envelope. Combine egg with water and seal corners of pastry dough. Repeat with each filet. Place filets on a greased baking sheet and put into a preheated 350-degree oven for 25 to 30 minutes, until pastry is puffed and golden brown. Serves 4.

KING'S CROWN DINING ROOM'S
SHRIMP WITH STONE-GROUND MUSTARD CREAM

Mustard Cream:

1 to 2 tablespoons stone-ground mustard	¼ teaspoon minced garlic
juice of ½ a lemon	¼ cup Parmesan cheese
2 to 3 dashes Tabasco sauce	¾ cup heavy cream
½ teaspoon horseradish sauce	

In a saucepan over medium-low heat, combine mustard, lemon juice, Tabasco, and horseradish until smooth. Add garlic and stir; add cheese and stir to combine. Slowly add cream, stirring continually.

Shrimp sauté:

3 ounces butter	1 scallion, sliced thin
20 jumbo shrimp	
¾ cup Mustard Cream (recipe above)	

Heat butter to medium-high in a skillet and sauté shrimp until about half-done. Add Mustard Cream and scallion and reduce until slightly thickened. Serves 4.

THE OLD CAPTIVA HOUSE
AT 'TWEEN WATERS
Captiva Island

THE OLD CAPTIVA HOUSE AT 'TWEEN WATERS

Because 'Tween Waters sits at the narrowest point of Captiva, stretching from the Gulf of Mexico to the bay, no matter where you sit in The Old Captiva House, you'll hear the peaceful rolling of the surf.

I watched guest after guest walk through the door of the restaurant and heave a sigh of relief. Its simple, clean, Old Florida charm just somehow seems to instill confidence. The wooden tables and chairs are a pristine white, and the remainder of the dining room is gently bathed in pale green and salmon tones. And if the surf isn't enough to lull you into relaxation, a pianist further sets the mood with semi-classical music.

During my visit, I learned that the most significant aspect of the island's past is its service as a holding place for prisoners. In the 1500s, a seventeen-year-old Spaniard named Juan Ortiz was held prisoner here by the Timacua Indians. He would have been burned alive had not the chief's daughter pleaded for his life. Later, she arranged Ortiz's escape to a friendly tribe, and the young man eventually joined Hernando De Soto's expeditions as an interpreter.

After sampling the Mussels Marinara, Oysters Rockefeller, and Captiva Bisque, I knew why the restaurant has been the recipient of numerous awards, including the Golden Spoon Award. I also sampled a piece of their homemade bread, which is honestly so good that it makes butter superfluous. I was served a crisp green salad with a special, creamy House Dressing. It was at this point that I learned the restaurant was built in 1913 as a house to tutor the children of John R. Dickey. In the 1920s, the house and surrounding cottages passed to the Price family, who allowed visitors to vacation here by invitation only!

When my entrées arrived, I learned that the Baked Grouper is uniquely prepared in a bag, which answers how it remained so moist. My Shrimp Scampi was also a treat, prepared with the right flavors to accent, yet not overwhelm, the fresh seafood taste. Conversations during this course led to my discovery that Charles and Anne Morrow Lindbergh, along with Pulitzer Prize–winning political cartoonist Ding Darling and wife, Penny, were among those invited by the Price family to vacation at Captiva. Darling holds the honor of having the island's wildlife preserve named after him.

After admiring original Ding Darling works on the dining-room walls, I agonized over which of the many homemade desserts to choose. I just couldn't say no to the moistest Carrot Cake going, or a taste of their Chocolate Bourbon Pecan Pie. You may favor their old-time Banana Cream Pie, which reminded me of banana pudding. And that's exactly the way dining and staying here is. The Old Captiva House at 'Tween Waters is one place, thankfully, where nothing is glitzy and new.

The Old Captiva House at 'Tween Waters is located at 15951 Captiva Road on Captiva Island. Breakfast is served daily from 7:30 until 10:30 a.m. Lunch is served from noon until 2:00 p.m. January through May. Dinner is served daily from 5:30 until 10:00 p.m. For reservations, call (813) 472-5161.

THE OLD CAPTIVA HOUSE'S
BAKED GROUPER

8 ounces of fresh grouper	¼ cup roasted leeks,
8-by-12-inch piece of	chopped
parchment paper	1 teaspoon lemon juice
2 tablespoons Dijon mustard	1 teaspoon white wine
1 teaspoon seasoned salt	sprig of dill

Place grouper on parchment paper. Spread mustard evenly over fish. Add seasoned salt and sprinkle leeks on top. Cover with lemon juice, white wine, and dill. Fold parchment paper over grouper and roll tightly. Bake at 475 degrees for 7 to 8 minutes. Serves 1.

THE OLD CAPTIVA HOUSE'S
CHOCOLATE BOURBON PECAN PIE

3 eggs
¼ cup plus 2 tablespoons
  butter, melted
¾ cup light corn syrup
½ cup sugar
2 tablespoons bourbon
1 tablespoon flour

1 teaspoon vanilla extract
1 cup pecans
1 unbaked pastry
  shell
1 cup semisweet
  chocolate morsels

Beat eggs in a large bowl until frothy. Add butter, beating well. Add syrup, sugar, bourbon, flour, and vanilla and beat well to incorporate. Stir in pecans. Pierce pastry shell on bottom and sides with a fork. Sprinkle chocolate morsels evenly over bottom of shell. Pour pecan mixture over top of morsels. Place pie in a preheated 350-degree oven and bake for 1 hour or until set. Yields 1 pie.

THE OLD CAPTIVA HOUSE'S
SHRIMP SCAMPI

½ teaspoon olive oil
6 jumbo shrimp, peeled
  and deveined
1 tablespoon minced garlic
¼ cup white wine
1 tablespoon unsalted
  butter

1 cup linguine,
  cooked
sprig of parsley for
  garnish

Heat olive oil in a skillet on medium-high for 1 minute. Add shrimp and garlic; toss gently for approximately 2 minutes, until shrimp starts to cook. Add wine and simmer as shrimp begins to pinken, then top with butter to finish. Serve over pasta with a touch of parsley for color. Serves 1.

VERANDA
Fort Myers

VERANDA

You won't hear the roar of cannons as you sit in the Veranda's tropical courtyard today. Nonetheless, this oasis was once the battleground for Seminole uprisings.

Due to white cattlemen's increasing need for land, the Seminoles were driven farther south. The cattlemen persuaded Congress to offer the tribes a bounty to move west. When it was clear that the offer was not amenable to the Native Americans, troops were sent in to quell the uprisings. During ensuing battles, a fort was built on the Caloosahatchee River and named after Major Myers, who lost his life during a tribal attack.

After the Civil War, Captain Manuel Gonzalez, the fort's former mail carrier, returned with his five-year-old son, Manuel, and operated a trading post. Years later, young Manuel built two adjacent houses at the corner of Second Street and Broadway—one for his family and the other for his mother. The houses were joined in the 1970s by Peter Pulitzer, son of the publishing giant, for his fishing buddy, Fingers O'Banion. O'Banion operated the houses as a restaurant and bar, as did Cloyd Pate after him. Paul Peden bought the buildings in 1979 and transformed them into one of southwest Florida's best restaurants.

The two Victorian Colonial Revival homes that make up the Veranda were built in 1907 and 1909. They are joined into a single structure by a country kitchen. The interior is elegantly decorated in muted green Victorian floral prints. At the side door of one dining room, you can see an herb garden, which supplies all the restaurant's fresh herbs.

I sat opposite a double-fronted brick fireplace in what was once part of the wraparound veranda. A large mound of fresh Oatmeal-Molasses Baked Bread was brought to me, along with homemade Pepper Jelly. My next delight was the Crab Bisque.

The Bourbon Street Filet is the kind of dish you'd expect to be served in heaven. The taste is opulent in its richness, and six ounces is more than enough for anyone. The varied Continental menu makes it difficult to choose among Norwegian

Salmon, Rack of New Zealand Lamb, and Vegetarian Ravioli, but who can resist fresh seafood in Florida? Marinated and Grilled Prawns over Linguine with Carbonara Sauce had a strong pull, but I settled on Cashew-Encrusted Grouper Meunière. When properly prepared, grouper is quite juicy. When smothered with crunchy cashews, it takes on a brand-new flavor.

For dessert, I had their famous Peanut Butter Fudge Pie, which tastes like a Reece's Cup, only better. But you might prefer one of their cobblers; the Blueberry is made in the old style, with no artificial ingredients. And the large servings are just one of many things that lend an old-fashioned appeal to this excellent restaurant.

The Veranda is located at 2122 Second Street at the corner of Broadway in Fort Myers. Lunch is served from 11:00 a.m. until 2:30 p.m. Monday through Friday. Dinner is served from 5:30 until 10:30 p.m. Monday through Saturday. There is live piano bar music Tuesday through Saturday. Facilities are available for the handicapped. For reservations (recommended), call (813) 332-2065.

VERANDA'S BOURBON STREET FILET

2 tablespoons butter
2 tablespoons vegetable oil
½ cup fresh mushrooms,
 chopped rough
½ teaspoon fresh garlic,
 minced
½ teaspoon fresh shallots,
 minced
½ cup green onions,
 chopped

cracked black pepper
 to taste
¼ teaspoon rosemary
¼ teaspoon thyme
2 6-ounce tenderloin
 filets
1½ ounces Kentucky
 sour-mash bourbon
2 tablespoons butter

In a large sauté pan, heat butter and oil at medium-high heat and mix to combine. Add mushrooms, garlic, shallots, onions, pepper, rosemary, and thyme and stir quickly. Place filets in pan and cook on all sides for 8 to 10 minutes, depending on thickness. Continually stir vegetables to keep from burning. When meat reaches desired doneness, add bourbon. Take care in lighting match to alcohol. Do not allow to boil. When flame dies down, add butter to sauce and stir. Serve filets topped with vegetable sauce. Serves 2.

VERANDA'S CASHEW-ENCRUSTED GROUPER MEUNIERE

4 6- to 7-ounce grouper filets	1 tablespoon parsley,
12 ounces cashews, crushed	chopped
(not ground)	1 tablespoon chives,
2 ounces clarified butter	chopped
4 tablespoons salted butter	juice of ½ a lemon

Trim filets. Spread cashews on a sheet of waxed paper or a flat dish. Place filets flesh side down into cashews. Place sauté pan on medium-high heat and add clarified butter. Let butter heat, but not to the smoking point. Carefully place cashew side of filets down into the pan and sauté until golden brown. Reduce heat to low, flip filets over, and cook an additional 2 minutes. Remove filets from heat, place on a sheet pan, and cook in a preheated 375-degree oven until done, 10 to 20 minutes depending on thickness of filets. In a separate sauté pan, melt 4 tablespoons of butter on medium-high heat. Stir in parsley and chives. Turn off heat and squeeze lemon juice into mixture. The butter should foam. Stir and spoon onto filets. Serves 4.

THE SKIPPER'S GALLEY
Fort Myers Beach

THE SKIPPER'S GALLEY

The Skipper's Galley came into existence in 1927, when Mrs. Anna Turner unceremoniously pulled her houseboat up on the beach of Estero Island and proclaimed it a restaurant and inn. She added a porch to the boat, where fresh seafood was served to guests.

That concept has changed through the years. Fresh seafood with sophisticated sauces has now been added to the menu, along with ambitious Italian dishes, and the inn and guest cottages that were part of the former Pelican Inn have faded into the past. The Pelican was purchased in 1988 by Alfredo Russo and Anthony Scialdone. But this isn't a tale about an unpretentious-looking houseboat. It's a story about the guests who have faithfully returned here, some for over twenty-five years. It is they who give this part of the island and Skipper's Galley their character.

In a way, this is a club—one to which I'd like to belong. When you dine at the Skipper's Galley, you become part of the old Pelican family and enjoy the company of Pelican friends, who refer to you as a "Pelicanite." And, as in all families, there are unwritten rules. An interesting one is the seating arrangement in the nautical dining room. You only get to sit by the window and watch passing boats silhouetted against the amber sunset when you have seniority. As the years roll by, repeat guests gradually move up. It's a bit like graduation.

I graduated quickly, not because of merit but because I came early. I was able to watch the sandpipers scurrying across the beach as an occasional sea gull dipped to search for prey. Even the pelicans made an appearance, and I'm told that one, named Phyllis, will come when called by a favored guest. I gleaned these tidbits while sipping a mood-altering Yellow Bird. With smooth Galliano mixed with an even smoother banana liqueur and fruit juices, this concoction is straight out of the Virgin Islands.

Since the former seafood restaurant has now taken on Italian dishes, I ordered the Calamari Salad, which is a cooked squid that's been marinated in olive oil and spices to enhance its natural offerings. You can order pizza or pasta along with a full spectrum of Italian entrées, or you can have a steak, but when I'm within toe-dipping proximity of the ocean, I'm going to have seafood. I was intrigued by both the Garlic Shrimp and the Snapper Almondine. Garlic gives the shrimp dish just the right amount of zip; this recipe is a quick one for home chefs to make. In the snapper dish, the sweet taste of amaretto combines with the flavor of the fish to make a memorably dainty delicacy.

After my tour of the restaurant, I was back at my unearned window seat beside the cypress walls. A frothy slice of Key Lime Pie was waiting. What a delicious way to end the day beside a Florida beach!

The Skipper's Galley is located at 3040 Estero Boulevard in Fort Myers Beach on Estero Island. Dinner is served daily from 4:30 until 10:00 p.m. Reservations are not accepted. For information, call (813) 463-6130.

THE SKIPPER'S GALLEY'S
GARLIC SHRIMP

2 tablespoons olive oil
2 tablespoons unsalted butter
20 jumbo shrimp
1½ cups button mushrooms, sliced
1 cup cherry tomatoes, halved

2 tablespoons fresh garlic, chopped fine
1½ cups white wine
juice of 1 lemon
salt and pepper to taste
linguine for 4, cooked

Heat olive oil and butter in a medium skillet and sauté shrimp for approximately 2 minutes. Turn shrimp and add mushrooms, tomatoes, and garlic. Sauté for 1 minute. Add wine, lemon juice, salt, and pepper. Reduce to desired consistency. Serve over linguine. Serves 4.

THE SKIPPER'S GALLEY'S
SNAPPER ALMONDINE

4 7-ounce red snapper filets
2 ounces olive oil
salt and pepper to taste
4 ounces sliced
  almonds

1½ cups amaretto
  liqueur
4 ounces unsalted
  butter

Brush filets with olive oil, salt, and pepper. Place on a greased baking sheet and bake in a preheated 350-degree oven for 7 to 10 minutes on each side, depending on thickness. Do not overcook. Place remaining olive oil in a small skillet over medium heat and sauté almonds until golden brown, stirring constantly, as they tend to burn. Add amaretto and light with a match. When flame dies down, reduce to a caramel consistency. Add butter a little at a time, stirring until sauce is smooth. Pour sauce over baked snapper. Serves 4.

THE BREAKERS
Palm Beach

THE BREAKERS

If there is one name that epitomizes the grandeur of Florida's early glory years, it is The Breakers. For kings and presidents, millionaires and socialites, conference delegates and families on summer weekend packages, The Breakers is a part of Florida's heritage.

It all started with Henry Morrison Flagler. When he built the railroad down the east coast of Florida, he built hotels along the way to attract the crowds. After fire destroyed the Palm Beach Inn, he built a more elaborate wooden structure called The Breakers in 1903.

For years, private railroad cars brought guests like the Rockefellers, the Astors, Andrew Carnegie, William Randolph Hearst, President Warren Harding, and the Duchess of Marlborough to winter at The Breakers. "The season" would end February 22 with the George Washington Birthday Ball, after which the guests would board the train in their finery and depart.

In 1925, The Breakers was destroyed by fire. A much more magnificent hotel was constructed on the same oceanfront site in less than twelve months of round-the-clock work by twelve hundred craftsmen and seventy-five European artists. The hotel was designed in the Italian Renaissance style by Leonard Schultze, architect of the Waldorf-Astoria. It's now listed on the National Register of Historic Places.

When you visit The Breakers today, you approach the imposing edifice via a long avenue that cuts through the green of golf courses and palm trees. Behind the sculptured fountain, patterned after the one in the Boboli Gardens in Florence, rise the twin belvedere towers and arches of the facade, inspired by the famous Villa Medici in Rome.

Inside, you see the artistry of fine European workmanship captured in tapestries, solid marble floors, frescoes, and vaulted ceilings. The Florentine Room's hand-painted ceiling is similar to the one in the Florentine Palace Davanzate. The adjoining Circle Dining Room, added in 1927, is painted with scenes of Italian cities and regions and is highlighted with a spectacular Venetian chandelier hanging from the circular skylight.

As one might expect in such a setting, the dining is formal and elegant. An award-winning wine cellar contains more than four hundred different vintages. The menu selections change according to the season. Included are such entrées as Sautéed Tournedos of Beef, Grilled Papaya Marinated Swordfish, Penne Pasta, and Cranberry-Coated Roast Pork Tenderloin.

Dinner is followed by dancing to the live orchestra. As you glide around the floor, you don't have to close your eyes and pretend you're in a palace ballroom; you only have to look up to know you're really there.—B. R. M.

The Breakers is located at One South County Road in Palm Beach. During the "high season," mid-December through April, the Circle Dining Room serves breakfast from 7:00 until 11:00 a.m. and dinner from 6:00 until 9:30 p.m. From May through early December, breakfast is served from 7:00 until 11:00 a.m. and dinner from 6:30 until 9:30 p.m. For reservations (required), call (407) 655-6611.

THE BREAKERS' KEY LIME PIE

1 8-inch pie shell
3 cups sweetened
   condensed milk
3 egg yolks

⅔ cup Key lime juice
1 cup whipped cream
lime slices

Prebake crust until light in color. Mix condensed milk and yolks until combined. Add juice and mix. Mixture will tighten as it sits. Pour into shell immediately. Bake at 350 degrees for 10 to 15 minutes; pie filling will still be soft. Refrigerate for 4 hours before serving. Garnish with whipped cream and lime slices.

THE BREAKERS'
HERB-CRUSTED RACK OF LAMB

1 half-rack of lamb
  (8 chops, bones cleaned)
salt and pepper
1 tablespoon prepared
  Dijon green herb
  mustard

breadcrumbs as needed
  (recipe below)

Season lamb with salt and pepper. Cook on a wire rack in a 500-degree oven for 12 to 15 minutes. Remove from oven and cool. Brush with mustard and roll in breadcrumbs. Return to a 350-degree oven to bring lamb to appropriate temperature, approximately 15 minutes for medium rare. Cut into double chops and serve. Serves 2.

Breadcrumbs:

1 cup cooked wheat berries
  (whole-grain wheat;
  couscous, brown rice,
  or orzo may be
  substituted)
1 tablespoon granulated
  garlic

1 tablespoon parsley
1 tablespoon cilantro
1 tablespoon basil
1 tablespoon rosemary
1 cup plain
  breadcrumbs
salt and pepper to taste

Chop half of the wheat berries very fine. Mix chopped wheat berries, whole wheat berries, and other ingredients.

ADDISON'S
Boca Raton

ADDISON'S

The brilliant, flamboyant architect Addison Mizner, darling of Palm Beach society, established the elegant Spanish style as the distinctive look of Florida's resort architecture in the early 1920s. In 1925, Mizner announced plans to create an entire Spanish-style city—Boca Raton. In November of that year, he built the first structure of his dream community—the Administration Building for the Mizner Development Corporation.

Patterned after El Greco's house in Toledo, Spain, the building incorporated Mizner's trademark barrel tile roof, adobe stucco walls, cypress doors and ceilings, handmade tile floors, and wrought-iron grilles. Addison Mizner used his "Administration Building" not only as his office and home, but as a place to entertain and dazzle Hollywood and New York celebrities and businessmen.

Today, that building houses a lovely restaurant, appropriately named Addison's. Rescued from demolition in 1986, the building has been beautifully restored at a cost of $9 million and is listed on the National Register of Historic Places.

Approaching the restaurant through the patio garden, you can hear the splash of water in the fountain and feel the cool of the huge banyan trees. Whether dining in the cloistered courtyard or the glass-walled veranda, you can savor the historic ambiance along with your meal.

Addison's specializes in fine Italian food. Its signature appetizer, "The Flavors of Italy," made of layers of crêpes, Italian meats, cheeses, and vegetables, is a delicious meal by itself. The pasta is all freshly made and includes Cannelloni filled with veal, spinach, and cheese and Penne Al Cognac, with ham, cognac, tomatoes, and cream.

Many traditional Italian favorites are offered, such as Osso Bucco, made of veal shanks in a tomato sauce, Gamberoni Scampi, shrimp cooked in garlic butter and white wine, and Eggplant Parmigiana. I thoroughly enjoyed my Scaloppine Di Vitello Al Marsala, medallions of veal in a Marsala wine and mushroom sauce, served with a house salad. The dessert cart contained an abundance of temptations, but I wisely chose to sample owner and Chef Joe Cordaro's award-winning "Tirami-Su."—B. R. M.

Addison's is located at 2 East Camino Real in Boca Raton. Lunch is served from 11:30 a.m. until 2:30 p.m. and dinner from 4:30 until 10:30 p.m. daily. On Sunday, a buffet brunch is served instead of lunch. Rooms may also be reserved for special events. For reservations, phone (407) 391-9800.

ADDISON'S OSSO BUCCO

⅓ cup olive oil
½ cup flour
6 veal shanks, cut 2 inches
   thick
1 cup chopped onion
1 cup chopped celery
1 cup chopped carrot

1 cup white wine
1 cup veal or chicken stock
½ cup chopped
   fresh parsley
4 cups chopped tomatoes
2 cloves garlic, chopped
salt and pepper to taste

Heat oil in a large pot. Flour the veal shanks. Brown the veal evenly over moderate heat, then remove from pan. In the same pan, sauté chopped onion, celery, and carrots until lightly browned. Return veal to pot, then stir in wine, stock, parsley, and tomatoes. Cover pot and simmer for 1½ hours, until meat is ready to fall from the bone. Add garlic, salt, and pepper. Serve over angel hair pasta or risotto. Serves 6.

ADDISON'S "TIRAMI-SU" ("Pick Me Up")

5 egg yolks
6 tablespoons sugar
10 ounces Marscapone cheese
1 cup espresso coffee
4 ounces Marsala wine

16 sponge lady fingers
   or 1 package Savoiardi
   Lady Fingers
powdered cocoa

Beat egg yolks and sugar together, then blend in cheese.

Mix coffee and wine. Dip lady fingers into coffee-and-wine mixture and place on a tray. Spoon on a layer of cheese mixture, then repeat with a layer of lady fingers as above. Spoon on another layer of cheese mixture, then sprinkle with powdered cocoa. Refrigerate several hours before serving. Serves 6 to 8.

LA VIEILLE MAISON
Boca Raton

LA VIEILLE MAISON When this Mediterranean-style mansion was built in 1928, it was a model home for celebrated architect Addison Mizner's residential development in Boca Raton. Today, it is a showcase of another sort—a showcase for some of the most exquisite dining in the state of Florida.

La Vieille Maison, "The Old House," is another of owners Leonce Picot and Al Kocab's famed restaurants, the others being in Fort Lauderdale and Monterey, California. Originally the home of Mizner's chief engineer, it had been turned into apartments when the restaurateurs bought the building in the mid-1970s. With the help of Fort Lauderdale architect David Martin and the decorating skills of Carolyn Picot and Al Kocab, the structure was restored to grandeur, and in 1976, the now-famous French restaurant opened.

When you walk through the wrought-iron gates of the two-story house, with its barrel tile roof and arched windows, you enter a tropical world of fountains and gardens. Continue and you step into a virtual designer's show house, with each high-ceilinged room decorated individually with antiques and *objets d'art*. Unmatched tables—oak here, marble-topped there—are set with fine crystal, china, and silver. And everywhere there are fresh flowers—mixed bouquets on the tables, sumptuous arrangements on the sideboards and buffets. Oil paintings, figurines, handcrafted chandeliers, imported tile on the fireplace—the eye is greeted with one delight after another in a profusion of harmoniously blended treasures.

When you're seated, you'll find your tuxedoed, European-trained waiter to be polite, knowledgeable, and gracious, gladly guiding even the most indecisive through the joys of ordering from a menu that soars to culinary heights. The wine list alone is awe-inspiring, drawing on a cellar that contains 120,000 bottles and represents an investment of more than a million dollars.

As is popular in many restaurants in France, the dinner is prix fixe. The set price per person includes five courses, with choices ranging from fresh trout flown in from Idaho, venison from New Zealand, and pheasant from Vermont to red snapper from Florida waters.

My husband, Tom, and I began our feast with Saucisson Chaud with Sauce Périgueux, a wonderful sausage mixed with pistachios and baked in phyllo pastry with a truffle sauce, and Escargots aux Petits Légumes, escargots poached in a creamy wine sauce with slivers of turnips, celery, and carrots—unforgettably delicious. Our main course, Trois Médallions, was a grand tour de force of sauces—a Lamb Noisette with Béarnaise, Beef Tournedo with Marchand de Vin, and Venison Tournedo with Grand Veneur.

The appealing cheese-and-fruit cart was followed by a salad with an excellent house dressing. And then came dessert! The Apple Sorbet was blissfully cool and refreshing. And the Crêpe Soufflé au Citron, with its raspberry sauce—featured on Julia Child's television show—was superb.

After such a meal, you can't help but linger, reveling in the romance of the setting, the perfection of the cuisine.—B. R. M.

La Vieille Maison is located at 770 East Palmetto Park Road in Boca Raton. Dinner seatings are at 6:00 and 6:30 p.m. and 9:00 and 9:30 p.m. every day. The restaurant is closed Memorial Day and Labor Day. For reservations (required), phone (407) 391-6701.

LA VIEILLE MAISON'S SALADE FLORIDIENNE

2 large, fresh pink grapefruit
1 cup sour cream
1 tablespoon brandy

3 tablespoons ketchup
12 ounces blue or
   stone crabmeat

With a sharp knife, peel the grapefruit and separate the sections so that no skin, pith, or pips remain. Mix some of the juice with a cup of sour cream. Add brandy and ketchup. Arrange the grapefruit sections on 6 plates. Place some crabmeat on the middle of each serving and spoon the sour-cream mixture on top of each. Serves 6.

LA VIEILLE MAISON'S POMPANO AUX PECANS

2 medium-size pompano
  (or 1-pound filets)
milk and flour for coating
2 tablespoons butter
salt and pepper to taste

8 pecans, shelled
  (6 crushed, 2 halved)
5 ounces Chardonnay
2 tablespoons heavy cream
fresh parsley for garnish

Fillet and skin the pompano. Dip them in milk, then in flour. In a 10-inch skillet, melt the butter on medium-high heat. When the foam subsides, arrange the filets in the pan and season with salt and pepper. Lightly brown one side about 2 minutes, then flip the filets over. Season again and spread the crushed pecans over and around the fish. After about 2 more minutes, add Chardonnay and sprinkle the cream over and around the fish. Reduce heat to low (the fish must not boil), cover the pan, and let the filets remain in the cooking liquids for a couple more minutes. To serve, place the filets on heated plates. Slightly reduce the juices left in the skillet and pour over the pompano. Decorate with pecan halves and fresh parsley. Serves 2.

CAP'S PLACE
Lighthouse Point

CAP'S PLACE

When the crusty old seafaring owner of Cap's Place was told that his remote, rustic restaurant was needed for a secret dinner party for President Franklin Roosevelt and Prime Minister Winston Churchill, he obliged. But Cap viewed the whole affair as a nuisance, what with all those Secret Service agents around, recalls Talle Hasis. Talle is the daughter of Cap's partner, Al Hasis, and she has run the restaurant for over twenty years.

Churchill had flown to Washington in the winter of 1942 to plan wartime strategies with FDR. When he came down with the flu, he sought the warmth of south Florida to improve his health. He stayed with Under Secretary of State Edward Stettinius, who owned a home across the Intracoastal Waterway from Cap's tiny island. When Roosevelt and General George Marshall arrived, they all went to Cap's Place to eat.

Cap's hasn't changed much since then. In fact, it's much the same as it was in the late 1920s, when a Spanish-American War veteran and fisherman, Captain Eugene Theodore Knight, started it all. Cap bought a dredging barge for one hundred dollars in Miami and towed it to a desolate island surrounded by mangrove swamp in what is now Lighthouse Point. He pulled it up on land and built a shack on top as a haven for fishermen. In the next few years, he added a house for himself and opened a restaurant accessible only by boat.

During the thirties, Cap's became a rumrunning restaurant and gambling casino. Cap opened the back betting room only for those diners he knew were well-heeled. Water glasses are stored today in the spaces which once held slot machines, ready to be dropped through a trapdoor if "the Feds" came.

The restaurant's rugged buildings, made of Dade County pine, with exposed beams and rafters, have weathered well. Much to the dismay of some old-time customers, the restaurant is now air-conditioned in the summer, though the windows are opened wide in cooler weather.

Historical photos and memorabilia line the walls. Of special interest is the mounted skin of a six-foot-long rattlesnake, shot on the island by Al Hasis just as it was about to strike Cap.

I watched a demonstration of how they peel the paper-thin edible portions of the sabal palm, or "swamp cabbage"—bought from a Seminole family in Okeechobee—to make their fresh Hearts of Palm Salad. After tasting this specialty, with its wonderful secret dressing, I could understand why it's so famous.

Oysters, clams, crabs, lobster, shrimp, scallops, and catch of the day—served broiled, deep-fried, pan-fried, sautéed, or poached in white wine—have been prepared for over fifty years. Though great pasta specials, fried chicken, and steak are offered, fresh Florida seafood is what Cap's is all about. That, and the adventure of a boat ride into the past.—B. R. M.

Cap's Place is located on an island a quarter of a mile north of Hillsboro Inlet, south of Boca Raton. You can catch Cap's launch at the boat dock at 2765 Northeast Twenty-eighth Court in Lighthouse Point. Dinner is served from 5:30 until 10:00 p.m. Sunday through Thursday and from 5:30 until 11:00 p.m. Friday and Saturday. For reservations (accepted), call (305) 941-0418.

CAP'S PLACE'S BLUEFISH DIJON

1 small bluefish filet (snapper, grouper, or trout may be substituted) juice of 1 or 2 lemons

2 tablespoons Dijon Sauce (recipe below) 1 tablespoon margarine

Marinate the fish in lemon juice for 10 minutes. Prepare Dijon Sauce. Dip fish, skin up, into sauce, then place on a heavy, flat iron skillet that has been greased with a pat of margarine. Cook fish on medium heat 5 to 10 minutes, until meat is no longer translucent and turns whitish. Flip fish over and spread Dijon Sauce on top. Warm a few minutes and serve. Serves 1.

Dijon Sauce:
**½ cup Dijon mustard
1 cup liquid margarine
1 teaspoon minced
  fresh garlic**

**1 tablespoon fresh
  lemon juice
1 tablespoon paprika**

151

Whisk ingredients together until orange-colored. Use for fish or broiled chicken. Store leftover sauce in a covered container in the refrigerator. Serves 8.

CAP'S PLACE'S SEAFOOD LINGUINE

Pasta:

1 pound linguine
3 cups water
3 tablespoons olive oil

½ tablespoon
fresh garlic

Cook linguine in boiling water to which olive oil and fresh garlic have been added. Cook al dente; remove from heat. Do not rinse or drain. (Add ice to stop further cooking if not using immediately.) Place pasta in warm casserole dishes, using a pasta scoop so some of the liquid drains out.

Seafood sauce:

5 tablespoons margarine
1½ tablespoons fresh garlic,
  minced fine
2 tablespoons fresh parsley,
  chopped
2½ cups milk
5 tablespoons all-purpose
  flour
2 pounds firm, white fish
  like grouper or dolphin

16 medium to large
  shrimp
1½ pounds fresh scallops
1½ tablespoons sherry
2 tablespoons fresh
  lemon juice
½ teaspoon paprika
salt to taste
Parmesan cheese to taste

In a saucepan, melt margarine and add garlic and parsley. Set aside. Warm the milk and add flour gradually, using a wire whisk to avoid lumps. Whisk until smooth and add to margarine mixture. Put saucepan on medium heat, but do not boil. Cook 5 minutes. Chop fish into bite-size morsels; peel and devein shrimp. Add raw seafood and cook 5 more minutes. Remove from heat. Add sherry and lemon juice. Blend in paprika and salt. Ladle mixture on top of cooked linguine. Sprinkle Parmesan cheese on top. Serves 6 to 8.

THE CHART HOUSE
Fort Lauderdale

THE CHART HOUSE Walking up to the Chart House in Fort Lauderdale, located in the historic Bryan Homes, you know that this is a special place even before you enter. The gracious tree-shaded yard along the New River, the lights shimmering on the water at night, and the two turn-of-the-century houses create an urban oasis of relaxed Old Florida.

In 1904, Fort Lauderdale founding father Philomen Bryan built these houses of rusticated concrete block for his sons Thomas and Reed, who owned the first electric, telephone, and water companies in Fort Lauderdale. The buildings are now the second- and third-oldest surviving structures in Broward County. They were declared historic landmarks and restored by the city of Fort Lauderdale in 1981.

They are now leased to the Chart House, a chain of restaurants that seeks out spectacular scenery and unique historic sites for its locations. Founded in 1961 in Aspen by Buzzy Bent and Joey Cabell, two world-class surfers whose equally strong passion for skiing took them to the slopes of Colorado, the Chart House group now numbers sixty-four restaurants. All are known for their quality food, friendly service, and casual, aloha-spirited atmosphere.

The Chart House in Fort Lauderdale has nautical touches throughout, with stained wooden moldings and ship models. Rattan furniture, Oriental rugs, and paddle fans add to the laid-back look. Located a block from the Broward Center for the Performing Arts, the restaurant is a popular stop for the theater crowd.

The menu offers many char-broiled selections, including Top Sirloin Steak, Filet Mignon with Béarnaise Sauce, and Chicken Breast Teriyaki. Prime Rib is a specialty. Seafood is always fresh and is "harvested without harm to other sea life." Salmon with Aioli Sauce and Shrimp Santa Fe—chili-coated and served with Blue Cheese Dressing—were especially tempting, as was the Wild Rice with Almonds and Pineapple.

For dessert, my husband and I couldn't resist splitting an order of Mud Pie. Enough for a party, it was fatteningly delicious!—B. R. M.

The Chart House is located at 301 S.W. Third Avenue in Fort Lauderdale. Dinner is served from 5:00 until 10:00 p.m. Sunday through Thursday and from 5:00 until 11:00 p.m. Friday and Saturday. For reservations (recommended), phone (305) 523-0177.

THE CHART HOUSE'S
BLUE CHEESE DRESSING

¾ cup sour cream
½ teaspoon dry mustard
½ teaspoon black pepper
½ teaspoon salt, scant
⅛ teaspoon garlic
   powder, scant

1 teaspoon
   Worcestershire sauce
1⅓ cups mayonnaise
4 ounces Danish
   blue cheese, crumbled

In a mixing bowl, combine first 6 ingredients and blend 2 minutes at low speed. Add mayonnaise and blend ½ minute at low speed, then increase speed to medium and blend an additional 2 minutes. Slowly add blue cheese and blend at low speed no longer than 4 minutes. Refrigerate for 24 hours before serving. Yields 2½ cups.

THE CHART HOUSE'S MUD PIE

½ package Nabisco
   chocolate wafers
½ stick butter, melted
1 gallon coffee ice cream

1½ cups fudge sauce
1 cup whipped cream
   for topping
½ cup slivered almonds

Crush wafers and add butter. Mix well. Press into 9-inch pie plate. Cover with soft coffee ice cream. Put into freezer until ice cream is firm. Top with cold fudge sauce; it helps to place fudge sauce in freezer for a time to make spreading easier. Store Mud Pie in freezer approximately 10 hours. Slice into portions and serve on chilled dessert plates. Top with whipped cream and slivered almonds. Yields 1 pie.

JOE'S STONE CRAB
Miami Beach

JOE'S STONE CRAB

Almost as long as there has been a Miami Beach, there has been a Joe's. Joseph Weiss, an asthmatic waiter in New York, moved to Miami in 1913 for his health. His short-order counter at Smith's Casino, a popular bathing spot, grew into a restaurant in 1918, when he started serving "shore dinners" on the wooden front porch of his family bungalow on the south end of Miami Beach.

In 1921, as Miami Beach entered the era of boom development, a visiting scientist asked Joe to cook a stone crab, a crustacean found in abundance but scorned by natives because of its odd taste and slimy texture. Joe cooked it, and then he chilled it, and that made all the difference. What had been an unpleasant-tasting meat when hot became, when cold, a sweet and succulent delicacy.

Joe started serving his cold Stone Crabs with melted butter and Mustard Sauce, and presidents, royalty, celebrities, millionaires, and just hungry folks have been queuing up ever since—and with no reservations accepted, lines are a tradition.

Along with culinary success has come media attention. Beginning in the 1930s with Damon Runyon, writers, critics, and gossip columnists have all covered Joe's, and television and movie directors have even used it in their scripts.

Joe's Stone Crab today is a big enterprise, with its own fishing fleet providing the restaurant with a ton of stone-crab claws a day and shipping more across the country and to Japan. Only the claws are harvested; the live crabs are returned to the water to regenerate new claws.

There is only one Joe's Stone Crab restaurant; there are no franchises, no branches, no clones. Located in a large stucco building with Mediterranean touches, the restaurant can seat up to four hundred at a time. The main dining room, built in 1930, is simply decorated, with terrazzo and black-and-white tile floors and enormous photos of the Weiss family on the wall. Mahogany woodwork, a wrought-iron chandelier, and a painted ceiling adorn the newer Garden Room.

Joann Sawitz Bass, Joe's granddaughter, is an elegant executive who oversees 170 employees with warmth and firmness. A cook herself from the age of twelve, she has a special test kitchen beside her office where she teaches the staff new dishes. She told me that it was her recipe, created when she was seventeen years old, that her father, Jesse, chose when he had to quickly find a Key Lime Pie after a Chicago restaurant critic raved about the one served at Joe's—when they offered none. It is now internationally acclaimed, and the recipe is a closely guarded secret.

Though Stone Crabs are Joe's trademark, the restaurant offers an abundant selection of other seafood as well, from fresh broiled snapper and pompano to shrimp, oysters, frog legs, and lobster. There are also salads and great vegetables, and even a smattering of meat entrées for the truly foolish.— B. R. M.

Joe's Stone Crab is located at 227 Biscayne Street in Miami Beach. Lunch is served from 11:30 a.m. until 2:00 p.m. Tuesday through Saturday. Dinner is served from 5:00 until 10:00 p.m. weekdays and from 5:00 until 11:00 p.m. Friday and Saturday. The restaurant is closed from mid-May to mid-October. Reservations are not accepted. For information, call (305) 673-0365.

JOE'S STONE CRAB'S VINAIGRETTE SALAD DRESSING

¼ cup chopped onions
or scallions
3 tablespoons minced parsley
2 tablespoons chopped
pimiento
1 hard-boiled egg, chopped
2 tablespoons minced chives

1½ teaspoons sugar
1 teaspoon salt
½ teaspoon red pepper
⅓ cup vinegar
¾ cup olive oil
½ cup capers (optional)

Mix all ingredients together. Serve on salads. Refrigerate leftover dressing. Yields approximately 2 cups.

JOE'S STONE CRAB'S
COTTAGE FRIED SWEET POTATOES

4 sweet potatoes
1 quart vegetable oil

salt to taste

159

Peel potatoes and cut them into slices that are as thin as potato chips, using the slicing blade of a food processor. Soak slices in ice water until you're ready to prepare and serve them. Heat the oil in a fryer or electric frying pan to 400 degrees. Blot the slices dry and fry them for 2 minutes, until crisp and golden brown. Remove with a slotted spoon and drain on paper towels. Sprinkle with salt and serve at once. Serves 4 to 6.

JOE'S STONE CRAB'S MUSTARD SAUCE

3½ teaspoons Colman's
  dry English mustard
1 cup mayonnaise
2 teaspoons
  Worcestershire sauce

1 teaspoon A-1 sauce
2 tablespoons light
  cream
⅛ teaspoon salt

Combine mustard and mayonnaise in a bowl and beat for 1 minute. Add remaining ingredients and beat until smooth and creamy. Serve as an accompaniment to fresh Stone Crab claws which have been cracked with a wide-headed mallet. Yields 1¼ cups.

JOE'S STONE CRAB'S GRILLED TOMATOES

4 beefsteak tomatoes
2 cups creamed spinach
  (your favorite recipe)
3 cups seasoned
  breadcrumbs

¾ cup melted butter
salt and pepper to taste
1½ cups mild
  cheddar cheese, grated

Cut each tomato into 3 thick slices and arrange on an oiled baking sheet. Combine creamed spinach with breadcrumbs, butter, salt, and pepper. The mixture should be thick. Spread each tomato slice with the spinach mixture and sprinkle with grated cheese. Place the tomatoes under a broiler and cook until cheese is melted and golden brown. Serves 4 to 6.

THE STRAND
Miami Beach

THE STRAND

The historic Art Deco District on Miami Beach has been transformed in the last few years from a struggling neighborhood of tired old hotels and rooming houses into an international mecca for the young, beautiful, and trendy. Sidewalk cafes and designer shops have been opened in recycled buildings, and throngs promenade along Ocean Drive, rollerblading, sunbathing, mingling, and enjoying the view of the Atlantic Ocean.

The Strand, a block back from the beach on Washington Avenue, was one of the first restaurants in the historic district to become a culinary presence to be reckoned with. In 1987, Gary Farmer and partners Irene Giersing and Mark Benck renovated what had once been the Famous Restaurant, a landmark deli.

Designed in 1934 by E. L. Robertson, the structure's facade boasts typical Art Deco touches like pelican capitals and a ziggurat parapet. Layers of linoleum and red carpeting were stripped away during the restoration work, leaving exposed the original terrazzo tile flooring. Dramatic lighting accentuates the interior Art Deco ceiling arches.

The blend of good food, friendly service, and cosmopolitan atmosphere has been an elixir for business success. In 1991, The Strand was purchased by three French investors—brothers Eric and Didier Milon and Charles Schreiner. Schreiner had been in the fashion industry in New York and had visited Miami often, with The Strand being his favorite restaurant. Under their management, The Strand has continued to be an internationally popular spot in which to be seen and to dine well.

When our party visited late one Wednesday night, the restaurant was pleasantly noisy, with music mingling with the conversation of a lively crowd. Tall, lean models, fashion photographers, artists, Europeans of all ages, and the young and trendy were still coming in at midnight.

Under the direction of Chefs Jeffrey Applebaum, Jose Tobon, and Sean Khouri, the menu offers a wide variety of American cuisine with a Continental touch. The Black Bean Soup we sampled was excellent, as was the Chilled Calamari over

Mixed Greens with a marvelously different Miso Vinaigrette. Though Meatloaf has been a Strand specialty for years, we couldn't resist ordering the Sautéed "Keys" Yellowtail Snapper with Mango–Black Bean Relish and Plantains, as well as the Fresh Thin Noodles with Mixed Seafood and Light Pesto Cream, both of which proved to be outstanding. The warm French Apple Tart, topped with cinnamon ice cream, was a perfect ending to a great meal and an exceptional evening.— B. R. M.

The Strand is located at 671 Washington Avenue in Miami Beach. Dinner is served daily from 6:00 p.m. until midnight, though the restaurant is open "until everyone leaves." For reservations (recommended), phone (305) 532-2340.

THE STRAND'S CHILLED CALAMARI OVER MIXED GREENS WITH MISO VINAIGRETTE

Miso Vinaigrette:
1 egg yolk
3 cups peanut oil
3 tablespoons red miso
  (a Japanese soybean paste)
3 tablespoons white
  or yellow miso

1 teaspoon fresh ginger,
  minced
2 cups champagne
  vinegar
salt and pepper

In a medium-size bowl, whisk the egg yolk until pale and thick. Drizzle the oil very slowly while constantly whisking, so that an emulsion is made between the egg and oil. Add the misos and ginger and mix well. Slowly add the vinegar and mix. Add salt and pepper to taste.

Mixed Greens:

Prepare a salad using a combination of lettuces such as Bibb, red leaf, green leaf, radicchio, frisee, watercress, and romaine. Any amount or variety may be used.

163

Chilled Calamari:

½ pound cleaned
   calamari (squid)
1 bay leaf
1 teaspoon cayenne pepper
1 teaspoon basil

1 teaspoon parsley
1 teaspoon oregano salt
1 cup white wine
2 cups water

Cut calamari into ½-inch-thick rings. Place all remaining ingredients into a pot and bring to a boil. Put the calamari in and cook only 2 minutes, no longer, or the calamari will become rubbery. Drain and chill.

Presentation:
chopped fresh chives
1 large tomato, cut into 8 slices, then cut in half

Mix the desired amount of greens and dressing in a bowl, then arrange on a plate. Place calamari rings on top of the greens. Drizzle a little more of the dressing over the calamari and sprinkle with chopped chives. Place four tomato slices around the plate. Serves 2 to 4.

THE STRAND'S GINGER STEAMED FISH

3 whole tomatoes, diced
1 bunch chopped cilantro
¼ cup lemon juice
1 cup white wine
2 stems of lemon grass
1 teaspoon lemon
   grass powder
2 leeks, finely
   julienned

¼ teaspoon minced
   garlic
12 slices of ginger
2 teaspoons olive oil
salt and pepper to taste
4 fluke, halibut, or
   flounder filets,
   6 to 8 ounces each

Four ovenproof dishes such as pie pans will be needed for this recipe. Place equal amounts of all ingredients except filets in each pan, arranging in a pile on top of one another. Place a filet over each pile and tuck the edges underneath. Wrap tightly with aluminum foil. Place in a preheated oven at 350 degrees for 10 minutes. Remove and serve. Serves 4.

FIREHOUSE FOUR
Miami

FIREHOUSE FOUR

Miami's oldest surviving fire station now houses one of the city's most popular restaurants, Firehouse Four. Constructed in 1923 as Fire Station No. 4, the Mediterranean-style building is listed on the National Register of Historic Places. The property is still owned by the city of Miami. In 1988, the empty structure was painstakingly renovated by developer John Meyer into a fine "dining saloon."

The beautiful pine and tile floors are original to the building. Old photographs and brass fire poles recall the days when firemen would leave Station No. 4 to rush off to a fire, sirens wailing on their truck.

Located a block off Brickell Avenue just south of the river in Miami, the restaurant is a lunchtime favorite for bankers, lawyers, and other professionals who work in the high-rise office buildings nearby.

The Friday-afternoon happy hour has become a popular tradition at Firehouse Four. In the former engine room, crowds mill around the handsome mahogany bar, enjoying the entertainment, drinks, and the complimentary buffet of Hot Wings, Meatballs, and Egg Rolls.

Firehouse Four is known for its aged beef, including Hamburgers, New York Strip, and Filet Mignon. For those who can take the heat, the flaming-hot Firehouse Chili will remind you of a four-alarm fire—good and hearty but not for the weak of palate. For those liking lighter fare, the excellent seafood is fresh daily, served either broiled, grilled, or sautéed. Salads are also a mainstay for many of the business lunch crowd.

I found the Key Lime Chicken—one of their most popular selections—to be delicious, with its blend of tart Key lime juice and cream sauce. And never one to pass up dessert, I adored Chef Julia Sammons's Firehouse Pie.—B. R. M.

Firehouse Four is located at 1000 South Miami Avenue in Miami. Hours are 11:30 a.m. until 10:00 p.m. Monday through Friday. The restaurant can be reserved for catered events on

Saturday and Sunday, when it is closed to the public. For reservations, call (305) 379-1923.

FIREHOUSE FOUR'S FIREHOUSE PIE

1 stick butter	1 cup walnut pieces
1 cup sugar	1 cup raisins
2 eggs	1 8- or 9-inch piecrust
1 teaspoon vanilla	(top and bottom)

Beat together butter, sugar, and eggs. Add vanilla, walnuts, and raisins and blend together. Pour into a pie pan lined with unbaked piecrust and top with piecrust. Bake at 375 degrees for 30 minutes or until golden brown. Yields 1 pie.

FIREHOUSE FOUR'S KEY LIME CHICKEN

Marinated chicken:

3 cloves garlic	1 cup oil
2 jalapeño peppers	10 skinless chicken breasts
¼ cup Key lime juice	

Chop garlic and peppers and mix with lime juice and oil. Marinate chicken breasts in this mixture for several hours or overnight. Grill the chicken over charcoal or on stove until done.

Key Lime Sauce:

1 pound unsalted butter	1 cup white wine
1 shallot	⅓ cup Key lime juice
3 jalapeño peppers	½ cup heavy cream

Soften butter at room temperature. Chop shallot and peppers. Put in saucepan with wine and lime juice and simmer. Add butter and boil 5 to 7 minutes to reduce, stirring continuously and being careful not to scorch. Add the heavy cream slowly over low heat, being careful not to add too much at one time. Stir to make creamy and smooth. Pour over chicken breasts and serve. Serves 10.

TOBACCO ROAD
Miami

TOBACCO ROAD

Liquor license 0001—the first in Dade County— is held by Tobacco Road. Built as a bar in Miami in 1912, the drinking establishment has led a wild and crazy life. A speakeasy during Prohibition, it was a reported hangout of Al Capone. It was also an illegal gambling casino raided by ax-wielding policemen. During World War II, it was off-limits to military personnel for encouraging "lewd and lascivious conduct." It was, as a sign in the present-day Tobacco Road says, "a constant source of anguish to law enforcement agencies."

When Patrick Gleber and Kevin Rusk were running a restaurant in an expensive suburban shopping center, they were approached by friend and realtor Michael Lattener to do a feasibility study on purchasing a "beat-up little dive." Though the immediate neighborhood had seen better days, the building was within a few blocks of booming Brickell Avenue, with all its gleaming new skyscrapers and international banks.

"Everyone thought we were crazy," Kevin Rusk recalls, but the three pooled their resources to purchase Tobacco Road. They redid much of the interior, though the front is still long and narrow and dark, and they made the rear patio into an appealing *biergarten*-type dining area.

Since then, they have been packing in evening crowds for their Chicago blues entertainment, and they have been drawing crowds of professionals at lunch for the great food.

Tobacco Road is well known for its Burgers—they freshly grind their own beef and make patties by hand—and for their cut-to-order French Fries. But the chef, John Kregg, a graduate of the Culinary Institute of America, goes far beyond that, offering homemade soups, salads, pasta, and seafood specials, as well as delicious desserts.

On the day I was there with friends, sitting on the terrace under an enormous old oak, I ordered a wonderfully prepared Mushroom Soup. The day's special, Escargots Provençale, served with linguine, was superb. So was the Curried Chicken Salad, judged the best in south Florida by a local magazine.

The owners are especially proud of their homemade Ice

170

Cream, offering interesting flavors such as Carambola and Cinnamon Chocolate. Though they had sold out of ice cream when I was there, I overcame my disappointment quickly when I tasted the Key Lime Pie and delicious Chocolate Tart.—B. R. M.

Tobacco Road is located at 626 South Miami Avenue in Miami. Hours are from 11:30 a.m. until 5:00 p.m. No reservations are necessary; for information, call (305) 374-1198.

TOBACCO ROAD'S ESCARGOTS PROVENCALE

1 tablespoon olive oil
6 to 8 escargots
1 teaspoon garlic, chopped fine
¼ green pepper, diced
½ tomato, peeled, seeded, and diced
1 teaspoon fresh basil, chopped
salt and pepper to taste
¼ cup white wine
6 ounces fresh linguine, cooked

Heat olive oil in a sauté pan. Add escargots and garlic and sauté lightly. Add peppers, tomatoes, and basil and sauté until tender but crisp. Add salt, pepper, and wine. Bring to a boil, then pour over linguine. Serves 1.

TOBACCO ROAD'S CARAMBOLA ICE CREAM

3 to 4 ripe carambola (star fruit)
2½ cups milk
2 cups heavy cream
1½ cups sugar
3 egg yolks
4 teaspoons vanilla

Cut the fruit into slices. Purée carambola in a food processor with half of the milk. In a mixing bowl, combine all the ingredients and mix with a whisk until the sugar dissolves. Pour the mixture into an ice-cream machine and let it run until the mixture is smooth, creamy, and thick, without a granular texture. Take the ice cream out of the machine and let it harden in the freezer, or eat as is. Yields ½ gallon.

TOBACCO ROAD'S SAUTEED CONCH STEAK WITH LIME BUTTER AND SAUTEED ALMONDS

6- to 8-ounce conch steak
salt and pepper to taste
¼ cup flour
2 tablespoons butter

1¼ cups white wine
1 tablespoon lime juice
1 tablespoon smoked
   almonds

Pound conch steak to tenderize. Season with salt and pepper and dust with flour. Melt 1 tablespoon of butter in a sauté pan and sauté conch about 3 minutes per side, until done. Remove steak from pan and keep warm. Add wine, lime juice, and almonds to the pan. Cook until the liquid reduces. Add the remaining tablespoon of butter and shake the pan until butter melts to make a sauce. Check seasoning and adjust if necessary. Pour over conch steak and serve. Serves 1.

CHARADE
Coral Gables

CHARADE

Much of the ornately carved furniture found in early Coral Gables homes, churches, and hotels came not from Old World Spain, but from the Granada Shops on Ponce de Leon Circle, the site of today's Charade restaurant.

When George Merrick planned his Mediterranean development of Coral Gables in the 1920s, he included a craft section to house and provide workshops for the craftsmen who would furnish the buildings of his community. Designed by Phineas Paist, these buildings were intended to be quaint counterparts of those in Italy and Spain.

The Granada Shops comprised a furniture store in the craft section. It was one of the success stories of Merrick's plan. Constructed in 1925, the building was owned by brothers Ralph and Leland Wilkins, who employed carvers from Spain, Italy, France, Germany, and Cuba. The family of Ralph Wilkins lived on the second floor, with a workshop and a large showroom downstairs. The barrel tile roof was damaged in the killer hurricane of 1926, which wiped out much of Miami, but the stucco building survived intact.

In 1939, the University of Miami purchased the building and used it for a Navy Officers Training School, then for band classes and rehearsals of the Music Department. It was a fraternity house and coffeehouse before being sold in the late 1950s to Lou Paoletti for an Italian restaurant. In 1976, a new owner did extensive renovation on the building, and in 1977, Charade was inaugurated.

With its awnings and flowers on the window sills and balcony, Charade is charming on the outside, and even more so on the inside. When you enter the main dining area, you are immediately struck with the mellowness of the old terra-cotta tile floors and the rich, dark beams of the two-story cypress ceiling. Oil paintings, chintz-covered chairs, a grand piano, hand-carved mahogany doors, and a cascade of potted palms create an atmosphere George Merrick surely would have appreciated.

While savoring the ambiance of a more tranquil era, one can indulge in appetizers like Escargots Bourguignone, Lobster Ravioli, and Carpaccio. Classic entrées like Lobster Thermidor, Steak Au Poivre, and Châteaubriand Bouquetiere are offered, along with Grouper Charade, served with a Pesto Cream Sauce, and Tortelloni with Spicy Shrimp. The Chocolate and Grand Marnier soufflés, a Charade specialty, offer a sublime culinary ending to the evening.—B. R. M.

Charade is located at 2900 Ponce de Leon Boulevard in Coral Gables. Lunch is served daily from noon until 3:30 p.m. and dinner from 5:30 p.m. until midnight. For reservations (suggested), call (305) 448-6077.

CHARADE'S ROAST
LONG ISLAND DUCK A LA "MALTAISE"

1 duck, about 3 pounds	¼ cup sugar
salt and freshly ground	2 teaspoons water
pepper	3 teaspoons red wine
1 fresh ginger root	vinegar
5 medium oranges	6 teaspoons dry
1 lemon	white wine
2 kiwi	1 cup chicken stock

Preheat oven to 400 degrees. Season duck inside and out with salt and pepper. Roast the duck for 1 hour. Peel ginger, oranges, lemon, and kiwi. Dice 3 oranges, half of the ginger root, and the lemon. Quarter the remaining oranges and kiwi. Slice the other half of the ginger very fine. Heat sugar and water in a saucepan until sugar caramelizes. Add vinegar and the diced fruits. Boil for 1 minute. Remove the duck from roasting pan; make sure all the juices inside the duck stay in the pan. Place duck aside. Add the wine to the cooking juices. Bring to a boil, scraping the bottom of the pan; reduce to half. Add chicken stock; reduce. Transfer the sauce to a small saucepan and return to a boil. Check seasoning. Add the remaining fruits to the sauce. Keep warm. Carve the duck, put it on a serving dish, and ladle the sauce on top. Serves 2.

CHARADE'S GRAND MARNIER SOUFFLE

4 teaspoons butter
5 teaspoons sugar
5 teaspoons milk
1 teaspoon cornstarch
3 teaspoons Grand
  Marnier liqueur

2 egg yolks
3 egg whites
pinch of salt

Preheat oven to 350 degrees. Coat bottom and sides of individual soufflé dish with butter, then sugar; shake off excess. Mix 2 teaspoons of sugar with milk. Bring to a boil, whisking constantly. Add cornstarch; continue whisking. When mixture thickens, remove from heat. Add Grand Marnier and egg yolks and let cool. Mix egg whites and salt and beat until stiff, then add remaining sugar and beat until smooth. Gradually and gently, add the egg-white mixture to the *cold* soufflé cream, using a rubber spatula; be careful not to "break" the egg whites. Put into soufflé dish. Bake for 20 to 25 minutes. Serves 1.

CHARADE'S SHRIMP SCAMPI WITH GARLIC BUTTER AND FRESH ARTICHOKES

2 teaspoons olive oil
4 extra-large shrimp
salt and pepper
4 fresh artichoke hearts,
  cooked
1 clove garlic,
  chopped

¼ cup white wine
4 ounces butter
4 teaspoons chopped
  parsley

Heat olive oil in a sauté pan. Season shrimp with salt and pepper. Add shrimp and artichokes to pan. When half-cooked, add garlic and wine; reduce by half. Add the butter, making sure to stir until the butter becomes part of the sauce; the result should be creamy. Add parsley. Serve with fresh pasta or rice. Serves 1.

RESTAURANT ST. MICHEL
Coral Gables

RESTAURANT ST. MICHEL

When Stuart Bornstein graduated from law school, he didn't hang out his shingle; he founded his own crêperie. In partnership with Alan Potamkin, he opened the Crêpe St. Michel in Coral Gables in 1974. Since then, he has expanded his dining establishment into a full restaurant, a bar and lounge, and an exquisite small hotel with individually furnished rooms. Polishing and perfecting along the way, he has created a nostalgic corner of European charm at his Hotel Place St. Michel.

Designed by Anthony Zinc, the Mediterranean-style three-story building features a dramatic entrance, balconies, and a rooftop tower. It was constructed in 1926 for offices and stores at a cost of twenty-five thousand dollars. Soon afterward, it became the Hotel Seville. During the 1960s, it was "modernized," with drop ceilings, fluorescent lighting, and Danish Modern furniture.

Stuart Bornstein has painstakingly restored the building to show off the original Spanish tile, the parquet floors, and the arched ceilings and windows. The French doors, the mahogany bar, the Art Nouveau lights from an old theater in Miami, the antiques, and the artwork all blend together in an Old World mélange.

The Restaurant St. Michel, just off the lobby of the hotel, is a casually elegant and popular dining spot, unintimidating enough for teenagers on special dates, yet sophisticated enough for international visitors.

The hardwood floors and wooden chairs and tables are reminiscent of French bistros. A brass teller's cage from an old bank accents the espresso coffee station. A white baby grand occupies a place of prominence, ready for the pianist who plays nightly and the jazz duo that plays for Sunday brunch.

Though manager Greg O'Leary emphasizes that the menu goes far beyond crêpes these days, covering a variety of French and Continental dishes, I still love what made the restaurant famous. Their Crêpes à l'Indienne, made with curried chicken topped with coconut, almonds, and chutney, is a personal favorite.

Appetizers range from Huîtres (oysters) Bienville and Steak

Tartare to Escargots de Bourgogne. Seafood entrées include Snapper au Basil, Homard au Gratin St. Michel (fresh Florida lobster in a spinach cream sauce), and Saumon Poché au Champagne et Oseille (poached salmon). Among the other entrées are Steak Poivre Crème, Canard au Cassis, and a delicious veal with wine, mushrooms, cream, and mustard called Escalopine de Veau Dijonnaise.

For dessert, you may order a Chocolate Mousse, a fresh Pastry, a Flambée, or Crêpes Sucrées. I'll take the Crêpe Chocolat Chantilly à la Mode, *s'il vous plaît.*—B. R. M.

Restaurant St. Michel is located in the Hotel Place St. Michel at 162 Alcazar Avenue in Coral Gables. Breakfast is served from 7:00 until 9:30 a.m. Monday through Friday. Lunch and dinner are served from 11:00 a.m. until 11:00 p.m. Monday through Thursday, from 11:00 a.m. until 1:00 a.m. Friday and Saturday, and from 6:00 until 11:00 p.m. Sunday. Sunday brunch is served from 11:00 a.m. until 2:30 p.m. For reservations (recommended), call (305) 446-6572

RESTAURANT ST. MICHEL'S
SALMON WITH GINGER CREAM SAUCE

4 6-ounce salmon steaks	juice of 2 oranges
1 cup white wine	6 ounces lowfat
3 laurel leaves	plain yogurt
dash of thyme	3 ounces cream cheese
2 shallots	salt and pepper
1 ounce fresh ginger	to taste
½ stick butter	

Place salmon in poaching pan and add white wine and enough cold water to cover fish. Add laurel leaves and thyme. Bring to a boil and immediately turn off the heat. Allow salmon to sit in the pan for 5 minutes. Meanwhile, sauté shallots and ginger in butter for 2 minutes, until golden. Add orange juice, yogurt, and cream cheese. Cook until creamy, stirring often. Season to taste. The sauce can be put in a blender to make it smoother at this point, if desired. Drain salmon, place on plate, and cover with sauce. Serves 4.

RESTAURANT ST. MICHEL'S CREPES A L'INDIENNE

2 shallots, chopped
½ stick butter
2 teaspoons curry powder
8 ounces heavy cream
4 ounces white wine
4 chicken breasts, skinned,
  deboned, and diced

4 Crêpes (recipe below)
¼ cup chutney
¼ cup shredded coconut
banana, apple, or
  mango slices for garnish

Sauté shallots in some of the butter. Add curry powder, cream, and 3 of the 4 ounces of wine. Cook the sauce 10 minutes. Sauté chicken in butter in another pan until golden. Add the curry sauce. Cook together 10 minutes, adding 1 more ounce of wine if the sauce is too thick. Reserve ¼ cup sauce. Place chicken with curry sauce in the middle of each Crêpe. Roll the Crêpes up, place on plates, top with some of the curry sauce, and garnish with chutney, coconut, and fruit slices. Serves 4.

Crêpes:

2 eggs
3 ounces flour

1 to 1½ cups milk
salt and pepper to taste

Stir the first 3 ingredients together and add salt and pepper if desired. Take ¼ cup of batter and pour onto a Teflon crêpe pan, covering the surface. Cook a minute or so and flip; cook another minute. Repeat until all 4 crêpes are done.

RESTAURANT ST. MICHEL'S
ESCALOPINE DE VEAU DIJONNAISE

12 2-ounce veal scaloppine
½ cup flour
1 tablespoon or more butter
3 ounces white wine
10 ounces heavy cream

½ cube beef bouillon
2 teaspoons Dijon mustard
4 fresh mushrooms, sliced
salt and pepper to taste

Dust veal with flour and sauté in butter for about 2 minutes. Remove from pan. Add wine, cream, ½ bouillon cube, mustard, and mushrooms and reduce over heat until creamy, about 3 minutes. Add salt and pepper if desired. Add veal to sauce to reheat, then serve. Serves 4.

IL RISTORANTE IN THE
BILTMORE HOTEL
Coral Gables

IL RISTORANTE IN THE BILTMORE HOTEL

For more than sixty-five years, the three-hundred-foot bell tower of the Biltmore Hotel has been a romantic landmark. Built by John McEntee Bowman and George Merrick, who felt his Mediterranean-style development of Coral Gables deserved a world-class hotel, the Biltmore was constructed in ten months at a cost of $10 million. For its January 1926 grand opening, trainloads of millionaires and celebrities came to enjoy lavish banquets, renowned orchestras, fox hunting, and gondola rides.

During the 1930s, oil tycoon Henry Dougherty kept the Biltmore in the news with dazzling water shows, tea dances, and golf tournaments that were frequented by Bing Crosby, Wendell Willkie, Rudy Vallee, Ginger Rogers, Judy Garland, and the Duke and Duchess of Windsor.

Used as an army hospital in World War II, the hotel later became a V.A. hospital, with ceilings lowered, rooms partitioned, and marble floors covered with linoleum. The federal government donated it to the city of Coral Gables in 1973, and the structure sat empty for years, home only to pigeons and vagrants.

Listed on the National Register of Historic Places, the building has undergone a $55-million restoration. Since its grand reopening as a hotel, the Biltmore has become a mecca for all those who glory in beautiful old architecture. The massive, columned lobby—with hand-painted ceilings, marble floors, mahogany paneling, and a baronial fireplace—the magnificent ballrooms, the loggias overlooking the golf course, and the famous pool where *Tarzan*'s Johnny Weissmuller once swam are all a source of much civic pride.

Il Ristorante, the hotel's formal dining room, is located on the ground floor, opening onto a courtyard accented with Spanish tile and a fountain. The restaurant is exquisitely elegant, with a marble entry, crystal chandeliers, gold-leaf ceilings, and chairs covered with tapestry and velvet. The spaciously arranged tables are set with damask cloths and fresh flowers. The ambiance is dignified and gracious, with live entertainment nightly.

Il Ristorante provided a beautifully appropriate setting to celebrate our very sophisticated daughter's fifteenth birthday. While piano music played in the background, we sampled Chef Donna Wynter's Bruschetta, a marvelous bread topped with tomatoes and a sauce. After an excellent Caesar Salad came a Lemon Sorbet to quicken the taste buds for the *pièces de résistance* to come: Filet of Tenderloin with Grapes and Peppercorn Sauce, and Rack of Lamb. For dessert, we had Tiramisu, an incredibly rich and delicious Italian dessert which has become a signature of Il Ristorante. Just as we all sighed in contentment, the waiter brought out the Chocolate-Covered Strawberries, set like gems on a crown of steaming dry ice. As we left, we were presented with yellow roses— a perfect ending to a memorable evening.—B. R. M.

Il Ristorante is located on the ground floor of the Biltmore Hotel at 1200 Anastasia Avenue in Coral Gables. It is open daily for dinner from 6:00 until 11:00 p.m. For reservations (recommended), call (305) 455-1926.

IL RISTORANTE'S FETTUCCINE DI GUISEPPE

2 tablespoons shallots, chopped fine
1 large clove garlic, chopped fine
1 tablespoon butter
½ teaspoon saffron threads
1 large leek, both white and green parts, thinly sliced on the bias
6 tablespoons very dry vermouth

¼ cup fish stock or fish bouillon
12 jumbo sea scallops (under-12-per-pound size)
1 cup heavy cream
salt and fresh-cracked white pepper to taste
¾ pound fettuccine
1 bunch French chives, chopped

In a hot pan, sauté shallots and garlic in butter; do not brown them. Add saffron threads and leeks, sauté briefly, and glaze with vermouth. Add fish stock, scallops, and heavy cream. Reduce slightly so that sauce will lightly coat the back of a spoon. Remove scallops so they do not overcook. Adjust seasoning with salt and white pepper. Cook fettuccine al dente, drain, and toss in sauté pan to coat noodles with sauce. Place fettuccine on plates and arrange three scallops on top of each dish. Garnish with chives. Serve immediately. Serves 4.

IL RISTORANTE'S
CARNE DI AGNELLO AL FORNO

¼ cup olive oil
4 double lamb chops
2 sprigs mint, chopped
1 bunch Italian parsley,
   chopped
4 tablespoons garlic,
   chopped fine
zest of 6 lemons (be
   sure the pith is
   removed from zest;
   don't blanch)

⅓ cup demi-glace sauce
(or can substitute
chicken broth,
double-strength,
reduced and thickened
with flour and water)
1 tablespoon unsalted
butter
salt and fresh-cracked
   black pepper

Place olive oil in a hot sauté pan and sear lamb chops on all sides until browned. Finish them in a preheated 450-degree oven until medium rare. In a mixing bowl, combine mint, parsley, garlic, and lemon zest. Mix thoroughly by hand. Reserve a small amount of this mixture, called gremolada, for garnishing serving plates. Heat demi-glace sauce in sauté pan and add gremolada. Add unsalted butter to give texture to the sauce; add salt and pepper to taste. Mirror the serving plates with the sauce; place two chops on each plate and garnish with reserved gremolada. Serves 2.

CAFE MARQUESA
Key West

CAFE MARQUESA

In 1886, a catastrophic fire raged through Key West, coming within 200 feet of the Victorian house James Haskins had just completed two years earlier. Saved by fate, the building would dominate the corner of Fleming and Simonton streets for over a century.

As time passed, a portion of the first floor of the home was lowered to street level and converted to commercial space, housing a grocery store, then a bicycle shop, then other small businesses. By the 1980s, the building was a five-dollar-a-night boardinghouse in great need of maintenance.

In 1988, the structure was saved from neglect when it was bought by preservationists Eric deBoer and Richard Manley. With much attention to authenticity, the two contractors transformed their property into a luxury hotel and restaurant.

Now listed on the National Register of Historic Places, the Marquesa is managed by Eric's wife, Carol Wightman. It has garnered a multitude of awards, both for the hotel's exquisite restoration and for the restaurant's wonderfully innovative cuisine.

To dine at Cafe Marquesa is to visit the home of a sophisticated friend. The space is intimate, with only fifteen tables, but not intrusive. It is chic, with art-covered walls highlighted by a large trompe l'oeil, but also warm and inviting. A mahogany bar, stone floors, and bay windows further enhance the bistro-style atmosphere.

And the food is a gourmet's dream, combining Florida and Caribbean ingredients with an international flair. Our dinner party tasted each other's main courses—Florida Lobster, Sautéed Yellowtail Snapper with Champagne and Papaya, Grilled Delmonico Steak with Roasted Elephant Garlic and Chimichurri, and Sesame-Encrusted Rack of Lamb with South African Barbecue Sauce—and we were left blissfully bewildered as to which was the most sublime.

Nor could we decide which dessert was the most inspired—Bread Pudding with Jack Daniels Sauce, Key Lime Napoleon, or Ginger Crème Brûlée. The only agreement we reached was that Chef Bob Carter's culinary skills had produced an evening of extraordinary dining.—B. R. M.

Cafe Marquesa is located at 600 Fleming Street in Key West. Dinner is served from 6:00 until 11:00 p.m. daily during the winter season and from 7:00 until 11:00 p.m. from Memorial Day to October 1. For reservations (required), phone (305) 292-1244.

CAFE MARQUESA'S GRILLED PORTABELLA MUSHROOMS WITH SOFT CORN POLENTA

Polenta:

2 cups milk
½ teaspoon white pepper
½ teaspoon nutmeg
1 teaspoon garlic, minced
¾ cup polenta meal
  or cornmeal

½ cup sour cream
2 tablespoons Parmesan
  cheese, grated

In a small saucepan, bring milk, white pepper, nutmeg, and garlic to a boil. In a slow, steady stream, pour cornmeal into boiling milk, whisking constantly. Reduce heat to simmer and continue stirring with a wooden spoon until mixture is soft and pulling away from sides of pan. Add sour cream and Parmesan; stir vigorously until incorporated. Adjust seasoning with salt, pepper, and nutmeg.

Portabella:

4 large Portabella
  mushrooms,
  10 to 12 ounces each
2 tablespoons balsamic
  vinegar
2 tablespoons fresh
  basil, snipped
1 tablespoon fresh
  thyme, snipped
1 tablespoon
  Worcestershire sauce

2 teaspoons minced
  garlic
1 cup chicken stock
  or water
1 cup olive oil
8 tablespoons
  Gorgonzola cheese,
  grated fine
½ cup tomatoes, peeled,
  seeded, and diced

Trim mushrooms at bottom and wash if necessary. Whisk

187

together vinegar, basil, thyme, Worcestershire, garlic, stock, and olive oil. Pour over mushrooms and let marinate for 30 minutes to 2 hours. Prepare charcoal grill. Remove mushrooms from marinade and allow to drain on plate for 1 to 2 minutes. Place mushrooms on rack over charcoal grill; turn occasionally. When mushrooms are soft, remove from heat. Heat 4 plates in oven and remove. Sprinkle 2 tablespoons Gorgonzola on each hot plate. Spoon ¼ of the Polenta in center of each plate; place mushroom on top of Polenta and sprinkle tomatoes around plate.

CAFE MARQUESA'S GINGER CREME BRULEE

6 cups heavy whipping
  cream
¼ cup fresh ginger, diced
12 egg yolks
1 cup sugar

1 tablespoon vanilla
  extract
granulated sugar for
  sprinkling

In a medium saucepan, bring cream and ginger to a boil. Turn off heat and let sit 5 minutes to infuse ginger. In a medium bowl, mix yolks, 1 cup sugar, and vanilla. Whisk egg mixture until sugar is dissolved and yolks are pale. In a slow, steady stream, pour hot cream mixture into yolks, constantly whisking to avoid curdling of eggs. Strain mixture through a fine sieve. Set 12 ramekins (8 ounces each) in baking pans with sides to hold water bath. Fill ramekins to within ¼ inch of top with cream mixture. Add enough hot tap water to pan to come halfway up side of ramekins. Cover pan loosely with foil, leaving ends tented. Place pan in preheated oven and bake at 325 degrees for approximately 25 minutes; the center of brûlée should wiggle when tested. Remove from oven, allow to cool for 15 minutes in water, remove from water, and refrigerate for 4 to 6 hours until completely chilled. To serve, sprinkle granulated sugar over each ramekin and place under broiler until sugar caramelizes. Remove and serve promptly. Serves 12.

LA CONCHA RESORT HOTEL
Key West

LA CONCHA
RESORT HOTEL

The six-story Hotel La Concha was the tallest and most up-to-date building in Key West when it had its grand opening in 1926. The same thing could be said of it now, after a $20-million renovation and a rejuvenated life as the Holiday Inn La Concha Resort.

Built of stucco, with copper screens and awnings over each window, the old hotel on Duval Street was long a source of community pride. For years, it hosted dances and parties and was frequented by celebrities and writers such as Ernest Hemingway, who lived in Key West for thirty years. Tennessee Williams wrote in his memoirs about staying in a "two-room suite on the top of the Hotel La Concha" with his beloved grandfather in 1946, while completing his play *A Streetcar Named Desire*.

Local residents have rejoiced to see the old hotel, which suffered years of decline and neglect, brought back to life. For the "fine rehabilitation" of the historic hotel and the "compatible new addition" that gives it more space and a pool area, La Concha received a rehabilitation award from the Historic Florida Keys Preservation Board.

La Concha's "Celebrities" is the gathering spot most evocative of days past, with its dark wood, mirrored columns, marble floors, and etched glass. In Key West tradition, it is open to the sidewalks of Duval Street, welcoming all to enjoy informal fare such as salads, sandwiches, pizzas, pastas, stone crabs, and shrimp. At sunset, happy hour moves to "The Top," the bar on the roof of La Concha, for a view of the glistening waters of the Gulf and the Atlantic and all of Key West.

More formal dining is offered in "Chops," the restaurant off the main lobby of the hotel. Done in mauve and blue tones, the room has a very stylized Art Deco look, with glass blocks accentuating a modern fountain and tall panels of glass overlooking an atrium of tropical plants.

True to its name, Chops specializes in oak-grilled meat. The Filet Mignon with Grilled Portobello Mushroom and the Marinated Lamb Chops with Roasted Garlic are fine examples. Also offered are Breast of Duck, chicken, and fresh grilled seafood. Appetizers now include Lobster Fritters rather than the traditional conch fritters, an environmental acknowledgement of the endangered status of conchs in the Keys.—B. R. M.

Holiday Inn La Concha Resort Hotel is located at 430 Duval Street in Key West. Breakfast is served in Celebrities from 7:00 until 11:00 a.m., lunch from 11:30 a.m. until 4:00 p.m., and dinner from 4:00 p.m. until midnight. Chops is open only for dinner; it serves from 5:30 until 10:00 p.m. and is closed on Monday. For reservations (suggested), phone (305) 296-2991.

LA CONCHA RESORT HOTEL'S HERB FETTUCCINE WITH LOBSTER AND ZUCCHINI SQUASH

3½ tablespoons unsalted
butter
1 small zucchini squash,
cut into quarters and
sliced in ¼-inch cubes
8 ounces herb fettuccine

¾ pound cooked
lobster meat
1½ tablespoons sour cream
½ teaspoon salt
½ teaspoon ground pepper
fresh parsley for garnish

In a large skillet, melt the butter over medium heat. Add the zucchini, reduce heat to low, and cook until zucchini is tender. Set aside. Bring a large pot of salted water to a boil. Add the fettuccine and cook until tender but still firm. Drain. Add the chopped lobster to the skillet; increase heat and cook, tossing until the lobster is warm through. Add the fettuccine; toss to combine. Turn off heat and stir in sour cream. Season with salt and pepper. Garnish with fresh parsley. Serves 2.

LA CONCHA RESORT HOTEL'S KEY LIME PIE

1½ cans (16-ounce size)
  sweetened condensed milk
⅓ cup Key lime juice
6 egg yolks

1 graham cracker
  pie shell
whipped topping

Combine condensed milk, Key lime juice, and egg yolks in a mixing bowl. Mix until completely blended. Pour mixture in pie shell and cook at 300 degrees for 10 minutes. Serve with whipped topping.

FLAGLER'S AT THE CASA MARINA
Key West

FLAGLER'S AT THE CASA MARINA

Henry Flagler, the millionaire visionary who brought the railroad down the east coast of Florida in the 1890s, completed his most ambitious undertaking in 1912, when he arrived on the first train to reach Key West. His Florida East Coast Railway's "Key West Extension" had just connected twenty-nine islands to the Florida mainland. It had taken seven years to complete, costing millions of dollars and hundreds of lives.

Flagler had planned to build a grand hotel in Key West, just as he had done in St. Augustine, Palm Beach, and Miami. But he died in 1913 at the age of eight-two before seeing the realization of his last dream.

It was not until 1921 that the elegant, two-hundred-room, Spanish Renaissance–style Casa Marina opened. It enjoyed prosperous years in the twenties, weathered storms and the Depression in the thirties, and was taken over by the navy in World War II for officer housing. Then, in October 1962, during the Cuban Missile Crisis, troops poured into Key West, and the Casa Marina became the home of the Sixth Missile Battalion. Barbed wire lined its beach, while on its oceanside lawn, missiles were pointed straight at Cuba, only ninety miles away. During the late 1960s, the hotel was used as a dormitory and school for the Peace Corps, and its appearance continued to deteriorate.

Finally, in 1978, massive renovations restored the Casa Marina for use as a Marriott Hotel. The lobby now gleams with its original pine floor, beamed ceiling, fireplace, arched windows, and French doors. Paddle fans, plants, and rattan furniture create a tropical, Old Key West ambiance.

The hotel's restaurant, Flagler's, is named in honor of Henry Flagler. It is much the same as it was in the 1920s, though extra dining levels have been added.

In the evening, waiters wear tropical Key West uniforms. A pianist plays for diners, who enjoy specials ranging from a delicious Blackened Key West Yellowtail to Rack of Lamb, Prime Rib, and Veal Piccata.

A rich array of desserts—like Key Lime Pie, Sabayon, and Flambéed Jamaican Bananas—is offered, as are exotic coffees.

I personally couldn't resist the Macadamia Nut Chocolate Cream Cheese Pie.

On Sunday, as is traditional in Key West, a big brunch is served on the veranda overlooking the Atlantic.—B. R. M.

Flagler's is located in the Casa Marina Resort on Reynolds Street on the ocean in Key West. Breakfast is served daily from 7:30 until 11:00 a.m. Lunch is served from 11:30 a.m. until 2:00 p.m. each day except Sunday, when brunch is served from 10:00 a.m. until 2:00 p.m. Dinner is served from 6:00 until 10:00 p.m. on weekdays and until 11:00 p.m. on Friday and Saturday. For reservations (suggested), call (305) 296-3535.

FLAGLER'S MACADAMIA NUT CHOCOLATE CREAM CHEESE PIE

Pie shell:

½ package Oreo cookies, crushed

6 tablespoons melted butter

3 ounces macadamia nuts, chopped fine

Mix all the ingredients together. Using the back of a spoon or your fingers, press the mixture against bottom and sides of a 9-inch pie plate. Bake in a 350-degree oven for 5 minutes. Cool.

Filling:

8 ounces cream cheese

6 ounces sugar

2 teaspoons vanilla extract

2 egg yolks

6 ounces semisweet chocolate, melted

4 egg whites

6 ounces macadamia nuts, chopped

16 ounces whipped dairy topping

Mix cream cheese, 4 ounces of the sugar, and vanilla in a blender or with an electric mixer until smooth. To this mixture, slowly add egg yolks and melted chocolate and blend until smooth. Set aside. Whip egg whites and 2 ounces of sugar into a meringue. Fold chocolate mixture into meringue. Fold in macadamia nuts, then dairy topping. Refrigerate until

195

mixture sets up, then spoon into cooled pie shell. Yields 1 pie.

FLAGLER'S CAESAR SALAD

2 small cloves garlic
3 anchovy filets
4 tablespoons olive oil
1 teaspoon Dijon mustard
dash of Worcestershire
  sauce
1 tablespoon wine vinegar

1 coddled egg
  (heated for 1 minute)
½ lemon
8 ounces romaine lettuce
¼ cup Parmesan cheese
fresh pepper to taste
½ cup croutons

Crush garlic cloves and rub garlic over a large salad bowl; remove the remains. In the salad bowl, use a fork to crush the anchovies into a paste, then add 1 tablespoon olive oil. Add mustard, Worcestershire sauce, 3 tablespoons olive oil, and wine vinegar. Break a coddled egg into the mixture and blend. Wrap the lemon in a cheesecloth, squeeze lemon into the mixture, and blend. Add the romaine lettuce and toss. Sprinkle Parmesan cheese over top and grind on some pepper. Add croutons and toss. Serve on chilled plates. Serves 2.

FLAGLER'S BLACKENED KEY WEST YELLOWTAIL

1 tablespoon sweet paprika
2½ teaspoons salt
1 teaspoon onion powder
1 teaspoon garlic powder
1 teaspoon cayenne pepper
1 teaspoon white pepper
1 teaspoon black pepper

½ teaspoon dried thyme
  leaves
½ teaspoon dried oregano
  leaves
6 10-ounce yellowtail filets
1 stick butter, melted

Thoroughly combine the seasonings in a bowl. Dip filets into melted butter and sprinkle the seasoning mix on generously. Heat a cast-iron skillet until extremely hot. Place filets in the hot skillet and cook until the seasoning mix on the fish looks charred. Turn filets over and repeat the process. Pour a small amount of butter over the filets and continue cooking until filets are firm. Serves 6.

LOUIE'S BACKYARD
Key West

LOUIE'S BACKYARD

Louie's Backyard in Key West is as big as all outdoors. It is the Atlantic Ocean with moored sailboats. It is a sea breeze and a full moon flirting with the lapping waves. It is a terrace landscaped with sea grapes and flowers, where the aromas of good food blend with the night air.

It is the backyard of a two-story frame house, complete with front porch and rocking chairs, built between 1909 and 1912 by Captain James Adams, a boatbuilder and wrecker. In 1971, Louis Signorelli started serving dinners here, beginning with twelve a night.

Owners Phil and Pat Tenney now serve 130 to 150 dinners nightly and have fifty-six employees. To the air-conditioned dining area of the original house, with its wooden floors and simple décor, they have added porches and terraces and decks. All overlook the water, with awnings and curtains that can be drawn to protect guests from rain showers.

Phil Tenney, once a woodworker, built the lovely bar himself. He has also supervised another addition; the second floor of the house has become a theater kitchen, where Executive Chef Doug Shook and *Chef de Cuisine* Susan Ferry create innovative specials daily. Wine tasting of expensive vintages by the glass is another attraction.

I was at Louie's on a night in May. Torrential showers had fallen that morning; the afternoon had been sunny and hot; the evening was heaven. As we sipped the excellent house wine, Sallye Jude, an ardent preservationist who restored Island City House in Key West, recalled the last time she was at Louie's—Prince Rainier had been entertained that night at the table next to hers.

Looking over the menu, I noted that the selections were indeed fit for a king, with Oven-Roasted Capon Breast with Thai Peanut Sauce, Rare Roast Loin of Venison with Sweet Onion and Ruby Port Sauce, and Sweet Soy-Glazed Grouper with Mango-Miso Sauce.

As we ate a Caesar Salad with Oyster Fritters and a mixed Lettuce and Asparagus Salad with Goat's Cheese, Phil Tenney joined us. He confirmed the story told around town that a bartender's dog, Ten Speed, had been a regular customer at Louie's for years, drinking a *crème de noyaux*—served in a champagne glass—at the bar every night. He added that when singer Jimmy Buffett once lived in the house next door, his cat Radar had also been a regular, preferring fish entrées.

While we enjoyed Roast Rack of Lamb and Norwegian Salmon with Mint, Cucumbers, and Black Beans, he told us of being raised by parents who worked for the State Department and of traveling around the world. "When I saw Duval Street," he said, "I thought, *This is it*, and I stayed." His is an experience shared by many converts to the Key West life. And his restaurant might just be adding to the number of converts.—B. R. M.

Louie's Backyard is located at 700 Waddell Avenue in Key West. Lunch is served daily from 11:30 a.m. until 3:00 p.m., with brunch (not a buffet) on Sunday. Dinner is served from 6:30 until 10:30 p.m. in the summer and from 6:00 until 10:30 p.m. during the season. For reservations (required), phone (305) 294-1061.

LOUIE'S BACKYARD'S HOT FRIED-CHICKEN SALAD WITH HONEY-MUSTARD DRESSING

Marinade:
2 jalapeño peppers
1½ tablespoons cayenne
  pepper
1½ tablespoons crushed
  red pepper flakes
salt and ground black
  pepper to taste

2 cups heavy cream
6 whole eggs
1½ tablespoons paprika
4 boneless, skinless
  chicken breasts

Remove stems and seeds from jalapeños and cut them into thin slices. Combine jalapeños, cayenne pepper, red pepper, salt, pepper, cream, eggs, and paprika and mix well. Cut the chicken into finger-size pieces. Add the chicken strips to the marinade and refrigerate 12 hours or more until ready to cook.

199

1 head romaine lettuce
1 head red leaf lettuce
Honey-Mustard Dressing
   (recipe follows)
4½ cups all-purpose flour
2 tablespoons salt
6 tablespoons
   black pepper
9 tablespoons red pepper
   flakes, crushed
3 tablespoons
   cayenne pepper
1 cup cooking oil
1 red onion, cut into rings

Wash and tear both heads of lettuce. (This may be done a few hours ahead, with the lettuce left in paper towels.) Put the salad greens in a bowl and toss with just enough dressing to lightly coat the leaves. Divide the leaves among 8 large, chilled bowls.

Remove the chicken from the marinade, allowing the excess to drip off. Combine flour, salt, black pepper, red pepper, and cayenne pepper. Roll chicken in this seasoned flour. Heat oil to approximately 350 degrees. Fry the chicken, turning it from time to time until it is light brown. Remove the hot chicken to paper towels and cut into bite-size pieces. Arrange the pieces over the greens and top the salad with 4 or 5 red onion rings. Serve immediately. Serves 8.

Honey-Mustard Dressing:
3 egg yolks
1½ tablespoons honey
3 ounces Creole mustard
   (or Pommery)
½ cup or less balsamic
   vinegar
1½ cups safflower oil
½ cup extra-virgin
   olive oil
⅛ cup roasted
   sesame oil

Combine all the ingredients and mix well. This dressing can be made 1 or 2 days ahead of time. Serves 8.

INDEX

APPETIZERS

BREADS

DESSERTS

Cakes:

Pies:

Miscellaneous:

Strawberries 1912, 1912 The Restaurant 12

"Tirami-Su," Addison's 143

ENTREES:
Fowl:
Chicken, Cabbage Key Restaurant 120

Chicken and Noodles, Hopkins Boarding House 4

Chicken and Yellow Rice "Ybor," The Columbia 104

Chicken, Avocado, and Bacon Salad, Lili Marlene's Aviators Pub and Restaurant 92

Chicken Stir-Fry, Mia's Cafe 32

Crêpes à l'Indienne, Restaurant St. Michel 180

Jamaican Chicken Nouvelle, The Great Outdoors Cafe 67

Key Lime Chicken, Firehouse Four 167

Poulet au Fromage, Le Pavillon 55

Roast Long Island Duck à la "Maltaise," Charade 175

Stuffed Cornish Hens Supreme with Wild Rice, Wakulla Springs Lodge 43

Meats:
Beef Cayenne, The Sovereign Restaurant 71

Bourbon Street Filet, Veranda 131

Carne di Agnello al Forno, Il Ristorante in the Biltmore Hotel 184

Escalopine de Veau Dijonnaise, Restaurant St. Michel 180

Filet Maison, The Greenhouse Restaurant and Lounge 35

Herb-Crusted Rack of Lamb, The Breakers 140

Longe de Porc au Poivre Vert, Jamie's French Restaurant 8

Osso Bucco, Addison's 143

Veal Chops, Chalet Suzanne 95

Veal Sorrento, The Lakeside Inn 83

Pasta:
Fettuccine de Guiseppe, Il Ristorante in the Biltmore Hotel 183

Herb Fettuccine with Lobster and Zucchini Squash, La Concha Resort Hotel 191

Seafood Linguine, Cap's Place 152

Seafood:
Atlantic Salmon, The Lakeside Inn 84

Baked Fish, Perry's Seafood House 15

Baked Grouper, The Old Captiva House at 'Tween Waters 127

Blackened Key West Yellowtail, Flagler's at the Casa Marina 196

Bluefish Dijon, Cap's Place 151

Cashew-Encrusted Grouper Meunière, Veranda 132

Chilled Calamari over Mixed Greens with Miso Vinaigrette, The Strand 163

Escargots Provençale, Tobacco Road 171

Fettuccine de Guiseppe, Il Ristorante in the Biltmore Hotel 183

Fish Island Hotel, The Island Hotel 76

Honey-Mustard Dressing, Louie's Backyard 200
House Dressing, Cabbage Key Restaurant 120
Key Lime Butter, Cabbage Key Restaurant 120
Miso Vinaigrette, The Strand 163
Mustard Cream, King's Crown Dining Room 124
Mustard Sauce, Joe's Stone Crab 160
Raspberry Vinaigrette Dressing, Lili Marlene's Aviators Pub and Restaurant 91
Remoulade Sauce, Perry's Seafood House 15
Shallot Balsamic Vinaigrette, Speaker's Corner 80
Tarragon Dressing, Lili Marlene's Aviators Pub and Restaurant 92
Tofu Salad Dressing, The Great Outdoors Cafe 67
Vinaigrette Salad Dressing, Joe's Stone Crab 159
Wasabi Dressing, The Maritana in the Don CeSar 112

SOUPS AND CHOWDERS
Black Bean Soup, Santa Maria 63
Caldo Gallego, Valencia Garden 108
Chili, Coley's 115
Clam Chowder, The Great Outdoors Cafe 68
"Claude's Bouillabaisse," Le Pavillon 56
Navy Bean Soup, Wakulla Springs Lodge 44
Navy Bean with Ham Soup, Busy Bee Cafe 27
Potato Scallion Soup, The Island Hotel 75

VEGETABLES
Beer Batter Fried Zucchini, Coley's 116
Cold German Potato Salad, Staff's 23
Cottage Fried Sweet Potatoes, Joe's Stone Crab 159
Fried Green Tomato Sandwich, Busy Bee Cafe 28
Grilled Portabella Mushrooms with Soft Corn Polenta, Cafe Marquesa 187
Grilled Tomatoes, Joe's Stone Crab 160
Squash Soufflé, Reececliff 99
Stewed Okra and Tomatoes, Hopkins Boarding House 3
Stuffed Eggplant with Crabmeat, Scotto's Ristorante Italiano 19
Sweet Potato Soufflé, Hopkins Boarding House 3
Zucchini Vegetable Pie, Mia's Cafe 31